HANDBOOK FOR THE PERSONAL ORIENTATION INVENTORY

HANDBOOK FOR THE PERSONAL ORIENTATION INVENTORY

Robert R. Knapp

EdITS publishers
SAN DIEGO, CALIFORNIA 92107

First Printing, March 1976

ISBN: 912736-17-8

Library of Congress catalog card number: 75-17256

CONTENTS

ILLUSTRATIONS

TABLES

FOREWORD

I am particularly gratified to write a note of appreciation and introduction to this volume. Robert Knapp has carefully and conscientiously compiled vast amounts of data that have accumulated on the POI during the past thirteen years. All of these data have been edited and summarized herein. I believe this volume will be particularly useful for researchers, clinicians, and students who are committed to measuring the positive aspects of growth in individuals and groups.

It has often been said that the POI represents the most primary solid body of research in humanistic psychology. For this I am most proud and grateful. I hope the users of this volume will share in this great continuing work.

Everett L. Shostrom
Director, Institute of Actualizing Therapy
Diplomate in Clinical Psychology
American Board of Professional Psychology

PREFACE

It has been over twelve years since the publication of Everett Shostrom's *Personal Orientation Inventory* (POI). During this time, the Manual has served as the major single source of information concerning the POI. Even though this manual underwent a minor revision in 1974 and again in 1975 it was not possible through that source to keep up with the fast accumulating research employing the POI. The latest *Tests in Print* (Buros, 1975) indicates references for the POI and ranks it fiftieth in terms of frequency of published research out of all personality instruments ranked.

Beyond the Manual, an early attempt to summarize and integrate the diverse content of this body of research data was presented in my 1971 report, *The Measurement of Self-Actualization and Its Theoretical Implications*, distributed by EdITS. While that publication fell far short of adequately integrating the fascinating web of data being generated from the POI, it did serve in part to answer the large number of inquiries concerning specific topics and samples to which use of the POI had been addressed. Also, it served as the foundation for the writing of this Handbook.

The most current bibliography for the POI, contained at the back of this volume, will still serve as the major guide to the interested researcher seeking original sources to research on specific topics. However, the availability of a broad overview of research results in a single source should serve a practical purpose to those interested in the concept of actualizing.

At the outset no claim is made to the extension of the theoretical model in the pages of this volume. Everett Shostrom's lead in this regard is acknowledged and it is assumed that those reading this volume will have already read his primary text and companion volume, *Actualizing Therapy: Foundations for a Scientific Ethic*. His dedication to communicating the concepts of actualizing is exemplary and will be recognized at all levels.

I wish to acknowledge in particular the contribution of those who have actively participated in bringing the research to its current stage of development. This present summary represents only a partial coverage of a research effort in its prime.

First and foremost are those authors whose published articles and dissertations are cited throughout and referenced at the back of the volume. Personal biases will, no doubt, be apparent in various sections. A major bias that hopefully shows throughout the volume is the necessity of confirming theoretical constructs through measurement.

Supportive of the system enabling these researches are the efforts of a number of individuals who must be recognized in this endeavor. Wayne Zimmerman guided much of the original data analyses upon which early publications were based.

Lila Knapp's statistical knowledge and constant interest in the concepts measured have contributed greatly to available analyses.

Of particular assistance in the latter stages of manuscript preparation were the efforts of Jack Allworth in summarizing areas of research and Dave Estrada in checking the accuracy of summary information and the clearness of expression. Bea Neher has typed the original manuscripts beginning with the first rough of the preliminary manual.

This book is dedicated to all those who labor in behalf of EdITS/Educational and Industrial Testing Service. Their efforts are reflected in the pages of this volume. Profiles reproduced throughout this volume, as well as other material taken from the manual, are reproduced with permission. This material is copyright by Educational and Industrial Testing Service.

Robert R. Knapp

San Diego
October, 1975

CHAPTER 1. THE PERSONAL ORIENTATION INVENTORY

The recent development of the concept of the *self-actualizing individual* has been accompanied by a rather substantial theoretical and speculative literature. The importance of this concept has been reiterated at all levels of society and is perhaps most clearly reflected in the observation by John Gardner (Jones, 1967), ex-secretary of Health, Education and Welfare, that "the basic American commitment is not to affluence, not to power, not to all the marvelously cushioned comforts of a well-fed nation, but to the liberation of the human spirit, the release of human potential . . . and self-fulfillment."

Until recently, due to the novelty and complexity of concepts of self-actualizing, little had been known about their structure and dynamic principles. Assessment of the conditions under which personal self-actualizing could be maximized, as well as the characteristics of institutions and treatments that fostered such growth, had to await the development of appropriate measurement techniques.

Recently, empirical research in this area has been facilitated through the development of an instrument for the measurement of personal self-fulfillment defined through concepts of self-actualizing. This instrument, the *Personal Orientation Inventory* (Shostrom, 1963, 1974), or POI, has stimulated extensive research into humanistic concepts and theory espoused by such writers as Maslow, Riesman, Rogers, Shostrom, and Perls. The concepts measured by the POI reflect an actualizing model that has been described as fast replacing the medical model for most counselors and therapists (Shostrom, 1972, 1973b; Shostrom, Knapp, & Knapp, 1976). The medical model, reflected in inventories such as the MMPI, stresses movement from "illness" to a mean of "normalcy," whereas the self-actualizing model stresses ways by which "normal" (well) people can become more effective and self-fulfilled. The switch to an educational model shifts the central focus of attention, that of responsibility, from the counselor to the client. When the client is "sick," the counselor must take the responsibility for effecting a cure, but when actualizing is the focus, the responsibility lies with the client to expand his or her own abilities to respond to life's situations. Counselors, therapists, and researchers studying the actualizing model have felt the need for an objective measure of the values and behaviors that are important in the development of the actualizing person. The POI was developed to meet this need.

The broad personal and social relevance of the value concepts measured, the interpretation of scales in terms of positive concepts of self-development, and the nonthreatening character of the items have been prime considerations in facilitating the application of the Inventory in a wide variety of settings. The importance of the availability of an instrument to measure humanistic concepts of self-actualizing can perhaps best be appreciated from a review of the diversity of the research stimulated by the POI. Such empirical research, aimed at verifying—and creating further insights into—the concept of the self-actualizing individual, necessarily had to await availability of relevant measurement instruments.

Since the initial validating studies, a large enough number of investigations have been conducted to enable Maslow (1971), in his posthumously published book, to state:

> In studying healthy people, self-actualizing people, etc., there has been a steady move from the openly normative and the frankly personal, step by step, toward more and more descriptive, objective words, to the point where there is today a standardized test of self-actualization. Self-actualization can now be defined quite operationally, as intelligence used to be defined, i.e., self-actualization is what the test tests. It correlates well with external variables of various kinds and keeps on accumulating additional correlational meanings. (p. 28)

In fact, the latest bibliography for the POI (found at the back of this volume) contains over 200 references, the results from many of which are integrated into this Handbook.

DESCRIPTION OF THE POI

The POI consists of 150 two-choice comparative-value-judgment items reflecting values and behavior seen to be of importance in the development of the self-actualizing individual. Briefly, such persons may be described as those who utilize their talents and capabilities more fully than the average person, live in the present rather than dwelling on the past or the future, function relatively autonomously, and tend to have a more benevolent outlook on life and on human nature than the average person.

In responding to the POI, the examinee is asked to select the one statement in each pair that is most true of himself. Clinically derived scales, comprising items logically grouped into two major scales and ten subscales, are used in comparing the examinee's responses to normative samples. The major scales are interpreted in terms of a *Time ratio* and a *Support ratio*. The Time ratio (time-competence/time-incompetence ratio) assesses the degree to which one is reality oriented in the present and is able to bring past experiences and future expectations into meaningful continuity. The Support ratio (inner-directed/other-directed ratio) defines relative autonomy by assessing a balance between other-directedness and inner-directedness. Other-directed persons tend to be dependent, whereas primarily inner-directed persons tend to be self-willed. A self-actualizing person transcends and integrates both orientations, and this transcendence expresses itself in an optimal ratio between other-directedness and inner-directedness.

The subsidiary scales purport to tap values important in the development of the self-actualizing individual: Self-Actualizating Value (SAV), Existentiality (Ex), Feeling Reactivity (Fr), Spontaneity (S), Self-Regard (Sr), Self-Acceptance (Sa), Nature of Man—Constructive (Nc), Synergy (Sy), Acceptance of Aggression (A), and Capacity for Intimate Contact (C).

While the POI has sometimes been described as a "forced choice" instrument (Raanan, 1973), such is not the case as reiterated by Shostrom (1973a). The Inventory format does not meet the criteria of a forced-choice instrument. Scale scores are *normative* rather than ipsative, with the score on one scale in general not being dependent upon responses to another scale. It is important for consideration of research design and statistical analysis to maintain this distinction. The POI item format is more properly described as "paired opposites," in which each concept is presented in terms of a positive and a negative statement of the continuum, or dichotomy, under consideration. Items of each scale are not paired with those of other scales; the scoring of each item remains independent. This may result, of course, in extreme profiles. For example, when compared against normative data, an individual can have high scores on the two major and all ten subscales or low scores on all twelve scales.

DEVELOPMENT OF THE POI

Shostrom's conceptualization of a measure of the self-actualizing person and his delineation of the initial scale constructs occurred during the summer of 1962, coinciding with Abraham Maslow's tenure as Visiting Fellow at the Non-Linear Systems, Inc. plant in Del Mar, California (at the invitation of the company's president, Andrew Kay).

The POI was developed to provide a standardized instrument for the measurement of values and behavior hypothesized to be of paramount importance in the development of the self-actualizing person. Initial development of the item pool was based on observed value-judgment problems seen by therapists in private practice. Further, these items were agreed to be related to the theoretical formulations and research of leaders in Humanistic, Existential, and Gestalt schools of therapy. Among concepts incorporated in the initial development of the POI were: Maslow's (1962,

1970) hypotheses about self-actualization; Riesman, Glazer, and Denny's (1950) system of inner- and other-directedness; May, Angel, and Ellenberger's (1958), as well as Perls' (1947, 1951), conceptualization of time orientation; and Bach and Goldberg's (1974) theories of acceptance of aggression.

As noted in the EdITS POI Manual (1974) and more completely developed in *Actualizing Therapy: Foundations for a Scientific Ethic* (Shostrom, Knapp, & Knapp, 1976), a number of authors in the humanistic area have contended that a self-actualizing individual is the goal of the psychotherapeutic process. Therapy may be viewed as a process of critically examining the irrational ideas and value orientations of the client. As Buhler (1962, pp. 30-31) has suggested, value orientations are definite existential judgments. Following Kluckhohn, she states that these value orientations symbolize the fact that affective-cognitive elements (value elements) and strictly cognitive elements are blended. A value orientation may be defined as a generalized and organized conception that influences behavior. It is a conception of nature, of man's place in it, of man's relation to man, and of the desirable and nondesirable as they may relate to man-environment relations and interhuman relations.

Ellis (1962, p. 41) notes that much of what is called emotion is nothing more or less than a certain kind of thought—biased, prejudiced, or strongly evaluative. Therefore, an affectively loaded idea about life may be properly defined as a value. Items in the Personal Orientation Inventory were designed to reflect value orientations that are commonly held and that are considered to be significant to a person's approach to living.

Items in the POI are stated both positively and negatively. Thus, the particular end-poles of the dichotomy in question are made explicitly clear. Authors of most other inventories have assumed that the reader knows the "opposite" of the statement in question—that it is implicit in the question. Perls (1947, p. 17), following Roget, has made it very clear that such is often not the case. Instead, opposites are dictated not by words but by their context. Thus, the same word often has several correlative terms, according to different relations in which it is considered. For example, both "receiving" and "taking" are opposed to the word "giving." The first correlative term refers to the persons concerned in the transfer. "Old" has both "new" and "young" as opposites, depending on whether it applies to living beings or to things. As Coan (1972, p. 293) has noted in his review of the POI, "the use of double-statement items makes the test seem a little monotonous, but it often provides the subject with a more clearly delineated choice than he would otherwise have. Its advantages seem to outweigh its shortcomings." It has been proven useful to explicity state the conceptual continuum in question, particularly in therapy.

THE POI SCALES

Scoring of the POI scales is accomplished in terms of the two major scales, Time Competence (TC) and Inner-Directed (I), and the ten subscales, described below. Since the major scales are viewed as being clinically interpretable in relative or proportional terms, they are frequently seen as ratios covering the two major areas important in personal development and interpersonal interaction, time orientation and support orientation.

Time orientation reflects the degree to which the individual lives in the present rather than the past or future. Self-actualizing persons are those living primarily in the present, with full awareness and contact, and full feeling reactivity. They are able to tie the past and the future to the present in meaningful continuity, and their aspirations are tied meaningfully to present working goals. They are characterized by faith in the future without rigid or over-idealized goals. They are "time competent." In contrast, the "time incompetent" person lives primarily in the past—with guilts, regrets, and resentments—and/or in the future—with idealized goals, plans, expectations, predictions, and fears. Figure 1 compares self-actualizing, normal, and nonactualizing persons on time orientations.

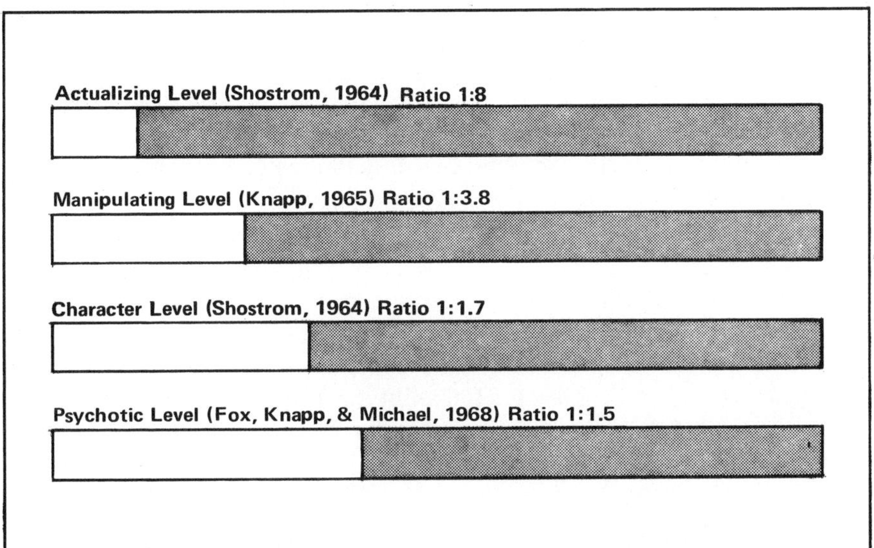

Figure 1. Comparison of Actualizing, Manipulative, Character, and Psychotic Groups on the POI Time Ratio.

Support orientation is designed to measure whether an individual's mode of reaction is characteristically "self" oriented or "other" oriented. Inner-, or self-, directed persons are guided primarily by internalized principles and motivations while other-directed persons are, to a great extent, influenced by their peer group or other external forces. Figure 2 compares self-actualizing, normal, and nonactualizing persons on support orientation.

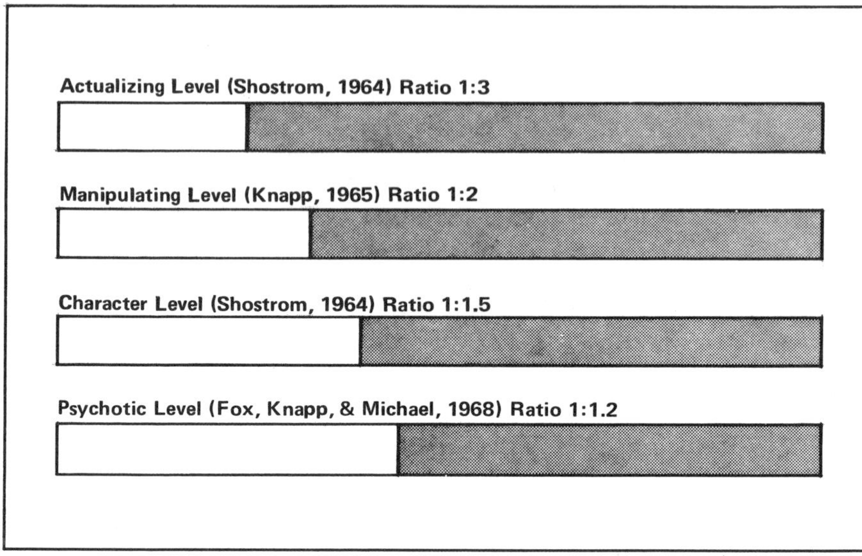

Figure 2. Comparison of Actualizing, Manipulative, Character, and Psychotic Groups on the POI Support Ratio.

Scores on each of the ten subscales are intended to reflect a particular facet important in the development of self-actualizing. These subscales may be defined as follows:

Self-Actualizing Value (SAV) measures the affirmation of primary values of self-actualizing people. A high score indicates that the individual holds and lives by values characteristic of self-actualizing people, while a low score suggests the rejection of such values. Items in this scale cut across many characteristics.

Existentiality (Ex) measures the ability to situationally or existentially react without rigid adherence to principles. Existentiality measures one's flexibility in applying values or principles to one's life. It is a measure of one's ability to use good judgment in applying these general principles. Higher scores reflect flexibility in application of values, while low scores may suggest a tendency to hold to values so rigidly that they become compulsive or dogmatic.

Feeling Reactivity (Fr) measures sensitivity or responsiveness to one's own needs and feelings. A high score indicates the presence of such sensitivity, while a low score suggests insensitivity to these needs and feelings.

Spontaneity (S) measures freedom to react spontaneously, or to be oneself. A high score measures the ability to express feelings in spontaneous action. A low score suggests that one is fearful of expressing feelings behaviorally.

Self-Regard (Sr) measures affirmation of self because of worth or strength. A high score measures the ability to like oneself because of one's strength as a person. A low score suggests feelings of low self-worth.

Self-Acceptance (Sa) measures the affirmation or acceptance of oneself in spite of one's weaknesses or deficiencies. A high score suggests acceptance of self and weaknesses, and a low score suggests inability to accept one's weakness. It is more difficult to achieve self-acceptance than self-regard, but self-actualizing requires both.

Nature of Man—Constructive (Nc) measures the degree of one's constructive view of the nature of man. A high score suggests that one sees man as essentially good and can resolve the good-evil, masculine-feminine, selfish-unselfish, and spiritual-sensual dichotomies in the nature of man. A high score, therefore, measures the self-actualizing ability to be synergic in one's understanding of human nature. A low score suggests that one sees man as essentially bad or evil.

Synergy (Sy) measures the ability to be synergistic—to transcend dichotomies. A high score is a measure of the ability to see opposites of life as meaningfully related. A low score suggests that one sees opposites of life as antagonistic. When one is synergistic one sees that work and play are not different, that lust and love, selfishness and selflessness, and other dichotomies are not really opposites at all.

Acceptance of Aggression (A) measures the ability to accept one's natural aggressiveness—as opposed to defensiveness, denial, and repression of aggression. A high score indicates the ability to accept anger or aggression within oneself as natural. A low score suggests the denial of such feelings.

Capacity for Intimate Contact (C) measures the ability to develop contactful intimate relationships with other human beings, unencumbered by expectations and obligations. A high score indicates the ability to develop meaningful, contactful, relationships with other human beings, while a low score suggests that one has difficulty with warm interpersonal relationships.

CHAPTER 2. VALIDATION AND APPLICATION IN ASSESSMENT AND RESEARCH

INDIVIDUAL THERAPY AND CLINICAL STUDIES

Early studies, many of which contained implications for the clinical application of the POI, were concerned with demonstration of the validity and reliability of this instrument. Shostrom (1964) demonstrated that POI scores significantly differentiated a sample of clinically nominated, self-actualizing individuals from a sample nominated as nonactualizing. This study provided important initial evidence for the validity of the POI in that the Inventory was shown to discriminate between individuals who have been observed in their life behavior as having attained a relatively high degree of actualizing, and those individuals who do not evidence such development. To test the POI's effectiveness in making this discrimination, the Inventory was administered to two groups—one of relatively "self-actualizing" and the other of relatively "nonactualizing" adults. Persons in these groups were carefully selected, each being the nomination of one of eighteen prominent, practicing, certified clinical psychologists (whose cooperation was secured through local societies of clinical psychologists.) Results of the analysis indicated that the POI significantly differentiated the groups on the two major scales and on nine of the ten subscales. All differences were in the expected direction. Profiles of these samples are presented in Figure 3.

In a series of studies examining responses of hospitalized psychiatric patients, Jack Fox has reported data relevant to the validity of the POI and relationship of age, sex, hospitalization, and ego factors to self-actualizing. In reports by Fox (1965a) and Fox, Knapp, and Michael (1968), a sample of 100 hospitalized psychiatric patients were found to be significantly lower on all POI scales than the nominated self-actualizing and normal adult samples reported by Shostrom (1964). The results were in concordance with the initial hypothesis—that a population hospitalized for psychiatric impairment would score significantly lower than a relatively self-actualizing group and a normal adult group—and the differences were in the expected direction as described. Further, all differences but one between the hospitalized sample and a clinically nominated *nonactualizing*, but nonhospitalized, sample were in the expected direction, and were not so great as between the hospitalized sample and the normal and self-actualizing groups. The POI profile for the hospitalized samples is presented in Figure 4.

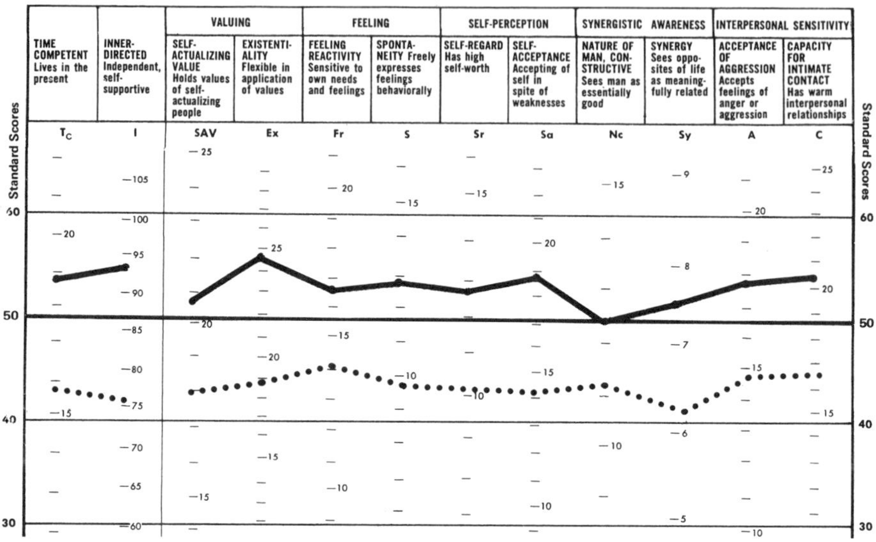

	Tc	I	SAV	Ex	Fr	S	Sr	Sa	Nc	Sy	A	C
Actualizing (—) (N=29)												
m	18.9	92.9	20.7	24.8	16.3	12.7	12.9	18.9	12.3	7.6	17.6	20.2
σ	2.5	11.5	3.6	3.5	2.8	2.9	1.9	3.5	2.2	1.2	3.1	3.4
Non-Actualizing (- - -) (N=34)												
m	15.8	75.8	18.0	18.9	14.3	9.8	10.2	14.2	11.3	6.2	14.7	16.5
σ	3.6	16.2	3.7	5.4	3.8	3.4	3.3	4.0	2.0	1.9	3.5	4.3

From Shostrom (1964)

Figure 3. POI Profiles for Nominated Actualizing and Non-Actualizing Samples.

The hospitalized group was depicted in terms of insufficient self-realization, inadequate orientation in time, and relatively nonautonomous functioning. The data do not indicate whether the POI scale scores reflect the premorbid level of functioning, or whether they are the result of changes in the psychological make-up that resulted in hospitalization. The findings did indicate that, as a group, the hospitalized population—as compared with other groups—tended to have fewer ego satisfactions, seemed more frustrated (and, consequently, more anxious, tense, and restless), and appeared to have less self-esteem. Because the patients were less reality oriented in terms of time orientation, and were hidebound, rigid, and conventional, the ordinary problems of living would rest more heavily on their shoulders and would thus tend to bring about internal tensions and distress.

While the major scales of Time Competence and Inner-Direction significantly differentiated the hospitalized sample from the clinically nominated nonactualizing sample, there was less clear-cut differentiation among these samples on some of the subscales. In addition to the nonhospitalized sample being depicted as more time competent and more inner-directed, other significant differences showed the nonhospitalized sample as being more able to react existentially without rigid adherence to principles (higher Existentiality), as showing more sensitivity of responsiveness to their own needs and feelings (higher Feeling Reactivity), as being more aware of the essential goodness of man (higher Nature of Man-Constructive), as being more able to accept aggressive tendencies within themselves (higher Acceptance of Aggression), and as having a greater ability to develop contactful, intimate relationships with other human beings (higher Capacity for Intimate Contact). Thus, as would be expected, the hospitalized group was more similar to the nominated nonactualizing group but yet displayed some clinically important differences. However, *all* POI scales significantly differentiated the hospitalized population from normal and self-actualizing samples.

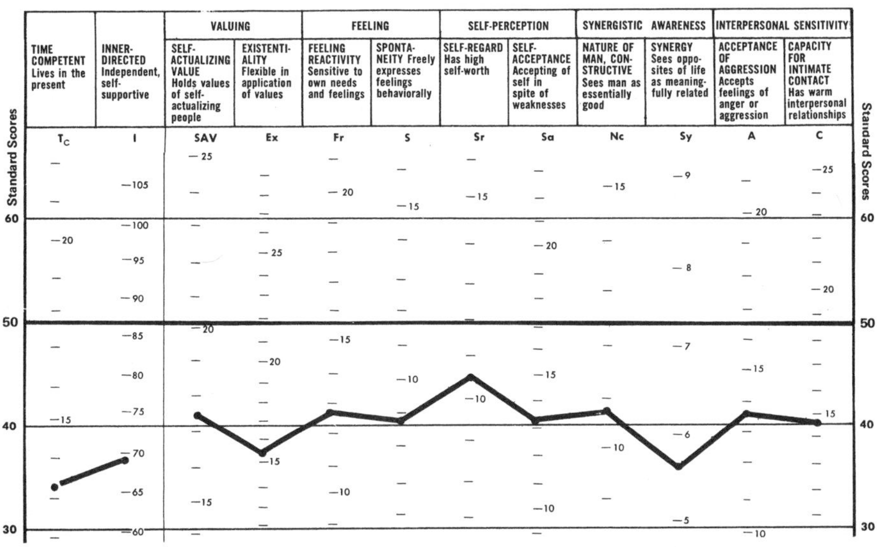

	T_C	I	SAV	Ex	Fr	S	Sr	Sa	Nc	Sy	A	C
m	13.4	69.0	17.3	15.2	12.7	8.9	10.5	13.1	10.6	5.7	13.3	14.7
σ	3.4	11.4	3.2	4.6	3.1	2.6	3.1	3.3	2.2	1.5	3.1	4.1

From Fox, Knapp and Michael (1968)

Figure 4. POI Profile for Hospitalized Psychiatric Patients (N=185).

In a study concerned with outpatients, Shostrom and Knapp (1966) found that all POI scales significantly differentiated a sample of outpatients just beginning therapy from those in advanced stages of psychotherapeutic progress. Profiles for these groups are presented in Figure 5. In this same study, POI scales were intercorrelated with MMPI scales for the male and female outpatient samples. Correlations, which are presented in Table 1, ranged in magnitude from .00 to -.67, the latter being in the male sample between the POI Spontaneity scale and the MMPI Social Introversion scale

(Si). The highest average *r* for both sexes was against the POI Inner-Directed scale. More significant relationships (twelve out of twenty-four *r*'s of .40 or greater, $p > .01$) were obtained with the Si scale than any other MMPI scale. The Si scale is presented not as a clinical scale (in the sense of being chiefly for use with hospitalized patients) but is purported to be widely used in counseling and guidance work. The comparatively high magnitude of correlations of POI scales against this scale (the average *r* being -.41) appears to support the contention that the POI is measuring attributes important in the development of harmonious interpersonal relationships within "normal" populations. The next greatest number of significant correlations were against the MMPI Depression scale (D), where eleven out of twenty-four *r*'s were above .40 and an average correlation of -.38 was obtained. Highest relationships with D were negative and against the POI scales of Inner-Directed, Acceptance of Aggression, and Self-Regard. These relationships support the contention that POI scales are tapping areas of "emotional morale," or psychological well-being.

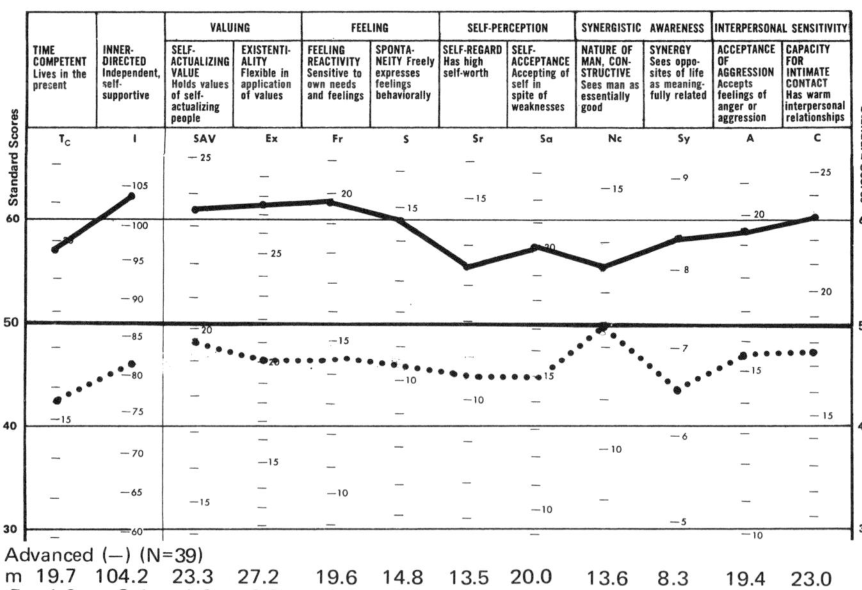

	Tc	I	SAV	Ex	Fr	S	Sr	Sa	Nc	Sy	A	C
Advanced (—) (N=39)												
m	19.7	104.2	23.3	27.2	19.6	14.8	13.5	20.0	13.6	8.3	19.4	23.0
σ	1.9	8.4	1.9	3.2	2.0	1.8	1.6	3.5	1.6	.8	3.0	2.7
Beginning (- - -) (N=37)												
m	15.6	81.2	19.6	20.1	14.5	10.7	10.7	15.0	12.4	6.7	15.6	17.8
σ	3.7	13.4	3.1	9.9	3.4	3.2	3.0	3.6	2.1	1.3	3.6	4.0

From Shostrom and Knapp (1966)

Figure 5. POI Profiles for a Beginning and an Advanced Outpatient Therapy.

TABLE 1

Correlation of Personal Orientation Inventory Scales Against MMPI Scales[1]

POI Scales	Symbol	MMPI Scales												
		Hs	**D**	**Hy**	**Pd**	**Mf**	**Pa**	**Pt**	**Sc**	**Ma**	**Si**	**L**	**F**	**K**
Time Competence	TC	–07	–47	–03	–31	–16	–23	–65	–52	02	–50	13	–55	50
		18	–31	02	–39	–36	–28	–31	–20	–02	–35	24	–40	44
Inner-Directed	I	12	–61	12	–18	02	–27	–53	–28	27	–62	–19	–50	51
		–03	–42	–01	–04	–22	–10	–25	03	28	–49	11	–17	36
Self-Actulizing Value	SAV	15	–33	04	–32	04	–21	–37	–22	36	–44	–05	–38	26
		–15	–35	–26	–21	08	–03	–22	–09	06	–35	–08	–31	29
Existentiality	Ex	23	–47	15	–12	03	–25	–40	–21	10	–47	–15	–45	47
		14	–37	13	05	–16	07	–15	14	34	–45	08	–03	31
Feeling Reactivity	Fr	06	–48	08	–02	03	–03	–33	–11	32	–46	–21	–31	28
		11	–36	09	02	–14	02	06	16	33	–28	–03	–03	23
Spontaneity	S	07	–49	05	–07	17	–07	–38	–21	33	–67	–18	–35	34
		–23	–33	–19	00	–05	–13	–33	–11	21	–38	06	–21	18
Self-Regard	Sr	20	–52	10	–21	11	–34	–49	–41	33	–60	06	–48	58
		–07	–48	–22	–15	–13	–10	–34	–17	16	–34	15	–41	41
Self-Acceptance	Sa	05	–52	18	–52	18	–20	–12	–28	–60	–35	–06	–45	–15
		–05	–32	11	–19	–31	–11	–27	–06	07	–45	04	–04	22
Nature of Man	Nc	04	–09	01	–25	–26	–23	–27	–19	12	–27	–10	–29	28
		01	03	11	14	–32	03	01	00	–05	–11	26	00	16
Synergy	Sy	22	–20	09	–36	–10	–15	–35	–31	08	–27	17	–51	34
		02	–22	–10	–32	–04	02	–22	–22	–11	–26	11	–27	32
Acceptance of Aggression	A	29	–53	46	09	07	–03	–38	–15	38	–61	–23	–36	52
		–04	–37	–08	–11	–12	–29	–33	–12	06	–27	–06	–10	–06
Capacity for Intimate Contact	C	06	–56	09	–10	04	–21	–38	–23	11	–46	–23	–38	48
		16	–25	16	15	–16	04	–02	07	40	–30	10	–10	28

[1] Decimal points omitted. Correlations for the beginning therapy group are shown in the top figure of each pair and for the advanced therapy group in the lower figure. From Shostrom and Knapp (1966).

COUNSELING STUDIES

The POI has been used extensively in counseling settings as a counseling technique, and some very important findings have been reported from research data generated under these conditions. Counselor level of self-actualizing, and the effect of this as an overall concept in the counseling process, has presented new implications for the theory of counseling.

Evidence of validity of the POI for measuring self-actualizing among a "normal" adult sample has been presented by McClain (1970b). A sample of thirty guidance counselors enrolled in an NDEA summer institute were rated by staff members in terms of self-actualizing. Ratings were highly reliable, with the mean correlation among raters being .77. Correlations between POI scores and the ratings ranged from .23 to .69, the latter being with the Inner-Directed scale. Other correlations significant at or beyond the .01 level of confidence were obtained with the Spontaneity (.53) and Self-Acceptance (.56) scales. The overall magnitude and significance of correlations obtained between POI scores and the highly reliable judges' ratings were offered by McClain as evidence that the POI does differentiate degrees of self-actualizing among normal adults.

Other evidence concerning the relevance of POI scales to counselor effectiveness has been presented in terms of correlations with ratings of counselor effectiveness among samples of clergymen. Jansen and Garvey (1973) related POI scales to supervisor ratings of counseling competency for a sample of eighty-eight clergymen in clinical training. High-rated clergymen obtained POI scores generally above the adult norm sample but somewhat below the nominated self-actualizing sample. Clergymen rated low obtained mean scores approximately those of the nonactualizing sample. Profiles for these samples are presented in Figure 6. Correlations between supervisor ratings and POI scales ranged from .02 to .49, with eight of twelve coefficients reaching significance beyond the .05 level of confidence. The greatest relationship was found with the Time Competence scale (r's = .49). Other scales significantly related to supervisory ratings were Inner-Directed, Self-Actualizing Value, Spontaneity, Self-Regard, and Nature of Man-Constructive. Considerable agreement was evidenced between supervisor and peer ratings of counseling competency (r = .64), and the POI scales were similarly related to these criteria, with seven out of twelve reaching significance beyond the .01 confidence for each criterion. Correlations against peer ratings were of the same approximate magnitude, ranging from .13 to .40 and presenting somewhat the same pattern.

In comparing those clerymen entering training (68% of whom were Roman Catholic and 32% Protestant) with the norm sample, Jansen, Garvey, and Bonk (1972) found the clergymen were significantly lower on three POI scales: Self-Actualizing Value, Existentiality, and Acceptance of Aggression.

At this point the question might be raised as to what beneficial effect the actualizing counselor brings to the counseling situation. Foulds (1969a, b, c) demonstrated the positive relationship between self-actualizing of

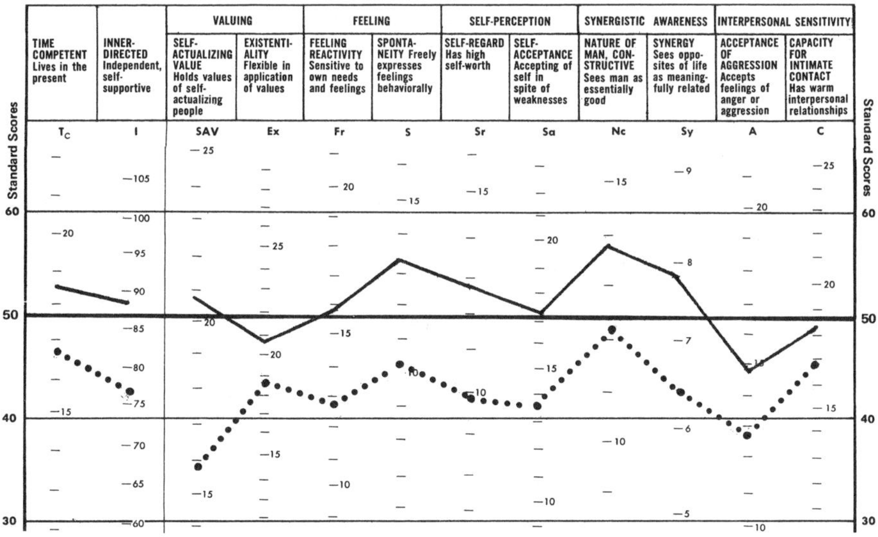

	Tc	I	SAV	Ex	Fr	S	Sr	Sa	Nc	Sy	A	C
High (—) (N=22)												
m	18.4	89.3	20.8	20.6	15.9	13.3	12.9	17.1	13.9	7.9	14.9	18.1
σ	2.8	10.4	2.4	3.9	3.2	3.1	2.3	2.8	1.3	1.3	3.8	2.9
Low (- - -) (N=23)												
m	16.6	76.6	15.9	18.8	12.9	10.1	9.9	13.7	12.2	6.4	12.7	16.9
σ	2.5	8.1	2.6	2.9	1.9	2.0	1.9	2.2	1.4	1.3	2.5	2.4

From Jansen and Garvey (1973)

Figure 6. POI Profiles for Clergymen in Counseling Training Rated by Their Supervisors for Clinical Competence.

counselors as measured by the POI, and their ability to communicate to the client the facilitative therapeutic conditions of empathic understanding, respect (or positive regard), and facilitative genuineness. Ratings of levels of these three characteristics among a group of thirty graduate students in a beginning supervised practicum were made by three sets of two judges each, all of whom were relatively sophisticated with respect to personality dynamics and psychotherapy. These ratings were correlated with the POI scores. The ratings of ability to communicate empathic understanding were significantly and positively related to six of the twelve POI scales ($p < .05$); ratings of the ability to communicate facilitative genuineness were significantly and positively related to ten of the twelve POI scales; and six POI scales were significantly and positively related to a total of the ratings of the conditions offered. The highest correlations (ranging up to $r = .55$) were against POI scales of Self-Actualizing Value, Feeling Reactivity, and Inner-Directed. None of the POI scales were significantly related to ability to communicate respect or positive regard. As Foulds notes, these findings suggest that the ability to sensitively and accurately perceive the inner "being"—or experiencing—of another human being, and to communicate this understanding to that person, is related to psychological well-being or self-actualizing as measured by the POI. Foulds further notes that the ability to be authentically real in a genuine encounter—without defensive "phoniness" or hiding behind the facade of a professional role—is also related to the POI measures of self-actualizing.

Foulds concludes by noting the significance of these findings to theories expounded by several writers, early among these being Rogers (1958), concerning the relationship between the psychological well-being of the counselor and his ability to provide facilitative conditions during counseling. Such theories hypothesizing the importance of psychological good health in the counselor receive research support from the data presented in this study.

In a follow-up study, questioning the practicability of assessing through measurement techniques the effectiveness of counselors, Winborn and Rowe (1972) failed to replicate Foulds' (1969c) results and reported only one significant correlation: that between the POI Synergy scale and Carkhuff's (1969) Respect, Positive Regard scale. The authors conclude by recommending replication of these studies to clarify the relationship between self-actualizing and the communication of facilitative conditions in counseling. A summary of correlations between counselor trainees, POI scores, and supervisors' ratings is presented in Table 2.

In an analogous study in the field of education, Coble and Hounshell (1972) found no relationship between level of self-actualizing of the teacher and student achievement in biology. However, in a more recent study involving 424 biology students and eighteen teachers, Coble (1973) found significant differences in self-actualizing between teachers whose students showed significant gains in critical thinking and those whose students evidenced nonsignificant changes in critical thinking. Those teachers whose students showed significant increases in critical thinking were significantly higher on the POI subscales of Existentiality and Capacity for Intimate Contact.

In a provocative but inconclusive study, Hood (1968), using a design wherein matches were made (on a rotating basis) between high and low self-actualizing counselors and high and low self-actualizing student clients, found the greatest amount of positive change when "low" counselors were matched with "low" clients. Although results in this study did not reach statistical significance, shortcomings of the research and the suggestions for strengthening the design might be expected to provide some challenging data for counseling theory.

Weinrach (1972) related the POI scores of twenty-three counselors with ratings of the guidance program based on responses of 1,658 eleventh-grade students. A highly significant correlation of .51 was obtained between Time Competence and overall ratings of the effectiveness of the guidance program. Thus guidance programs that exhibited high effectiveness as rated by students tended to be administered by counselors who received high Time Competence scores. Looking at subscores from the rating scale, the more self-actualizing the counselor the higher the rating assigned to (1) the guidance program activities and provisions, (2) the identification of the

TABLE 2

Correlations of POI Scores for Counselors in Training with Supervisors Ratings

POI Scales	McClain, 1970[1]	Jansen, Bonk, & Garvey, in press[2]	Foulds, 1969c[3]	Winborn & Rowe, 1972[4]	Graff & Bradshaw, 1970[5]
Time Completence	40*	49**	27	–26	53[6]
Inner-Directed	69**	26*	49**	–01	34
Self-Actualizing Value	41*	37**	55**	–07	45
Existentiality	43	06	39*	04	14
Feeling Reactivity	45	19	46**	04	18
Spontaneity	53**	34**	40**	09	45
Self-Regard	36	31**	33*	01	20
Self-Acceptance	56**	39**	33*	–16	35
Nature of Man–Constructive	23	38**	26	–09	05
Synergy	32	39**	29*	–12	07
Acceptance of Aggression	42*	15	33*	11	32
Capacity for Intimate Contact	42*	02	41**	03	09

[1]Supervisors ratings of self-actualization (N=30).

[2]Supervisors ratings of self-actualization (N=88).

[3]Supervisors ratings of facilitative genuineness (N=30).

[4]Supervisors ratings of facilitative genuineness (N=50).

[5]Supervisors ratings of dormitory assistant effectiveness (N=71).

[6]Significance levels not presented.

*Significant at the .05 level.

**Significant at the .01 level.

counselor as a source of assistance, and (3) the overall success of the guidance program.

Related to the effects of the counselor role are the studies of dormitory assistants who are frequently employed in quasi-counseling positions in college and university residence halls to assist students in making the most of their college experience. Graff and Bradshaw (1970) and Graff, Bradshaw, Danish, Austin, and Altekruse (1970) have presented evidence that the POI is highly related to dormitory-assistant effectiveness as measured by ratings of students and personnel deans. Canonical correlations revealed the primary predictor variables to be the Inner-Directed,

Self-Actualizing Value, Spontaneity, and Acceptance of Aggression scales of the POI. Obtained vectors were .65, .41, .73, and .36 respectively. The authors conclude that the POI may have practical value as a tool for the selection of dormitory assistants.

Tapp and Spanier (1973) also found that college students vounteering to work as telephone counselors in a suicide prevention service were significantly higher than nonvolunteers on the two major POI scales, Time Competence and Inner-Directed, as well as subscales on Self-Actualizing Value, Spontaneity, Self-Acceptance, and Capacity for Intimate Contact.

An interesting comparison of techniques for the teaching of interpersonal relationship skills by university campus paraprofessionals has been reported by Archer and Kagan (1973). Interpersonal communication skills training groups led by undergraduate residence-hall leaders using an interpersonal-process-recall videotape-feedback training model were compared with groups using a limited-structure encounter-group model and with no-treatment control groups. Participants in the interpersonal-process-recall videotape-feedback groups scored significantly higher than did the encounter or control group participants. The major conclusions reached by Archer and Kagan were (1) that a structured video-feedback/simulation film training model can be used successfully by undergraduates to teach interpersonal skills to other undergraduates, (2) that an interpersonal-process-recall model appears to be more effective than a less structured encounter-developmental group when used by paraprofessionals, and (3) that, with training and supervision, undergraduates can function as group leader-trainers for interpersonal-communication-skills groups. Archer and Kagan note that the most important implication of the study is that, due to the relative greater success of the structured groups as compared with the less structured encounter-developmental group model, paraprofessionals may operate more effectively when considerable structure is provided.

Underachievement

A number of studies in counseling situations have contributed to an understanding of the interrelationship between self-actualizing and underachievement. Leib and Snyder (1967), in a study of group counseling with college underachievers, examined the interaction of underachievement and scores derived from pre- and post-course administration of the POI. Underachievers were divided into two treatment groups: group discussion or lecture. While no significant differences were found between treatments, significant increases for the total experimental sample were obtained in grade-point average and in self-actualizing as measured by the POI Inner-Directed scale. Leib and Snyder suggest theoretical implications deriving from these data: In line with Maslow's concept of the development of self-actualizing, the special attention afforded the experimental group may have met lower needs of belongingness, love, and esteem, releasing these individuals for further personal development or greater self-actualizing.

In a related study, Pearson (1966) investigated the effects of different group guidance processes on pre- and post-course administrations of the POI in a freshman orientation course. Four groups were used, employing small-group interaction, group participation with a leader, regular leader-planned classes, or the control conditions with students exempted from the class. The hypothesis was that increases in self-actualizing would be greatest for students exposed to a permissive, group-directed form of guidance permitting intense interaction between students. A significant F-ratio was obtained for the POI Existentiality scale, favoring the group-directed approach. All significant *t* ratios also favored this approach, and grade-point average was significantly higher for the group. In terms of theoretical importance, Pearson felt that the results reflected an increased self-acceptance generated by the confidence placed in students' ability to find effective solutions to problems and that this is a part of a psychological "chain reaction" described in Rogers' (1951, pp. 481-533) theory of personality and behavior.

Another approach to examining trends in the relationship between self-actualizing and ability is to compare the POI scores obtained from samples of different ability levels. Weber (1970) has presented data obtained from ninth, tenth, eleventh, and twelfth grade girls showing that, among samples of high school students grouped according to ability, POI scores are generally lower among the lower-ability groups. In examining the pattern of differences at each grade level between the four ability classifications used, significant differentiation was most frequently obtained on scales of Time Competence, Nature of Man, Existentiality, and Synergy. Interpretation of these differences in terms of significant POI scales suggests that the higher-ability students tend to live more in the present, have a more constructive view of the nature of man, tend to be more flexible in the application of rules and principles, and more readily see the dichotomies of life in meaningful relationship.

In general, correlations computed between POI scales and the grade-point average criterion, when ability is not partialed out, have been positive and of comparative low magnitude, although the conclusions reached in different studies seem to vary with the type of sample employed. As is true of certain other noncognitive scales correlated with academic success, the POI scales might be expected to make a contribution in multiple-regression analyses in predicting GPA. Stewart (1968) reported a significant correlation of .36 between GPA and the POI Capacity for Intimate Contact scale. Other correlations reported were .28 and .26 respectively against the Nature of Man and Acceptance of Aggression scales, although in the sample of thirty-one college sophomores, juniors, and seniors, these did not reach statistical significance. Johns (1970) reported significant positive correlations of .27 and .30 respectively between GPA and Spontaneity and GPA and Self-Acceptance in a male freshman sample. A significant correlation of .24 was reported between GPA and Time Competence in the female sample.

Le May and Damm (1968) used the POI to study the value orientations of college underachievers who had volunteered to receive group counseling centered on academic and personal problems. In contrasting POI scores for the underachiever sample with those obtained from a matched group of academically successful students, the latter were significantly higher on the major Inner-Direction scale and five subscales: Existentiality, Feeling Reactivity, Self-Acceptance, Acceptance of Aggression, and Capacity for Intimate Contact. The largest difference appeared on the I (Inner-Directed) scale, indicating that the academically successful group was more inner-directed—more able to effectively direct their own lives relatively independent of peer pressure and urging than the underachievers. Another large difference occurred on the Capacity for Intimate Contact subscale, indicating that the academically successful group tends to be more capable of developing intimate relationships with others. Le May and Damm note that, taking into account the Feeling Reactivity, Acceptance of Aggression, and Capacity for Intimate Contact pattern, the underachievers manifest more social alienation and withdrawal, while the academically successful group tends to display more healthy interpersonal relations.

Leib and Snyder (1968) related the POI Support ratio (Inner/Other ratio) to criteria of academic overachievement and underachievement obtained from a ratio of predicted to obtained college GPAs. In their analysis, based on 354 students, no significant relationships were found between these ratios. A possible further hypothesis was offered: Self-actualizing, as reflected in the Support ratio, and achievement may not be directly related but perhaps are related secondarily through separate relationships with other variables. To further examine this hypothesis, Le May (1969) controlled for aptitude in his investigation of the relationship of self-actualizing to college achievement as measured by GPA. Using the POI Inner-Directed scale as the index of actualizing, and partialing out the effects of intellectual ability, correlations were computed against grade-point average in a sample of 205 male and 206 female undergraduate college students. Each of the two sex groupings was further subdivided into three equal sized subgroups, with aptitude test scores defining low, middle, and high intellectual-ability groups. Correlations between the Inner-Directed scale and GPA, with intelligence partialed out, were not significant for either the male or female samples among the high-ability or the low-ability subgroups. However, among the middle-ability students, significant correlations of -.25 ($p < .05$) and -.30 ($p < .01$) for the male and female samples respectively were obtained. That the relationship is negative suggests that activities resulting in obtaining good grades may not be seen as self-actualizing by the average student. Le May noted that the data for these three groups support the theory that the academic success of bright and dull students may be determined more by intellectual factors than is the case with average-ability students.

The finding that, among middle-ability students, the POI I scale was negatively correlated with GPA supports the conclusion of Leib and Snyder

(1968), cited above, that these two concepts of ability and self-actualizing are not directly related but may be related secondarily through separate relationships with other variables. As Le May (1969) notes, this explanation appears acceptable since evidence reported previously by Le May and Damm (1968) suggests that the I scale differentiates achievers and underachievers matched on aptitude. Thus, intellectual ability would appear to be a potentially important moderator variable in the analysis of relationships between actualizing and college achievement.

EVALUATION OF THE EFFECTS OF ENCOUNTER GROUP EXPERIENCE

The gaining popularity and widespread use of encounter group experience as a force for personality change is attested to in the number of recent publications on this topic. The encounter group concept is one of the most current innovations, and perhaps the most challenging to techniques of measurement, among personal growth methods. As Rogers (1968) has indicated:

> The intensive group experience is one of the most rapidly growing phenomena in the United States . . . because people . . . have discovered that this group experience alleviates their loneliness and permits them to grow, to risk change. The encounter group brings persons into real relationships with persons.

Intensive group experiences have been offered under many different names and in a wide variety of settings. "T-group," "sensitivity training," "human relationships training," and various laboratories and workshops in leadership, management, and education are, for present purposes, considered together under the general descriptive title "encounter group experience." Since the first T (training)-group experience—held in Bethel, Maine in 1947—use of the technique has grown to the point where persons in practically every segment of society and every area of the country have access to such experiences—not to mention those foreign countries where it has been introduced. Such groups now function in industry, the church, the military, governmental agencies, and in educational institutions from the public secondary school through the university. Often times groups are homogeneously composed of individuals from similar backgrounds with similar goals or problems (such as management trainee groups or Synanon) but in other instances are composed of volunteers or clients of widely divergent personal characteristics.

Maslow (1970), in considering group therapy techniques, has said:

> A final implication of our approach of psychotherapy is a greater respect for group therapies as well as T-groups etc. . . . If ordinary therapy may be conceived of as a miniature ideal society of two, then group therapy may be seen as a miniature ideal society of ten . . . in addition we now have empirical data that in-

> dicate that group therapy or T-groups can do some things that individual psychotherapy cannot. (p. 263)

However, the question as to whether such techniques do in fact yield enduring positive personality change (Gibb, 1971) or actually result in psychological damage in some cases (Yalom & Leiberman, 1971) has only recently been subjected to objectively quantified assessment.

The *Personal Orientation Inventory* has been a major instrument used in these studies. In fact, in a recently published review of instruments in human relations training, Pfeiffer and Heslin (1973) have noted:

> The POI, perhaps more than any other instrument described in this book, measures the things talked about by people in human relations training. For this reason it is an excellent training device. It awakens people to important dimensions of life and ways of viewing the world and themselves that they may well not have considered previously. (p. 100)

Compilations of studies in which the POI has been used to evaluate the effects of encounter may be organized in a number of ways. For example, of the fifteen studies considered by Knapp (1973), seven dealt with adult samples, seven with college-student samples, and one with high-school students. Eight studies incorporated a control group while seven did not compare results with a control-group sample. Sample sizes, an important factor in statistical interpretation, ranged from fourteen to 135, with results of eleven of these studies based on responses from more than thirty subjects.

Perhaps of greater importance in the review of these studies are the effects of such variables as length of time over which the changes are evaluated and comparisons of effects of different encounter techniques. Before undertaking studies evaluating effects of such variables upon outcome of the encounter group experience, relevant measurement techniques were required. Availability of the POI has greatly accelerated research in this area.

ACTUALIZING LEVELS OF THOSE SEEKING ENCOUNTER EXPERIENCE

A frequently asked question is "Who seeks the encounter experience?" Noll and Watkins (1974) compared differences on POI scores between thirty-nine college males and forty females who participated in encounter groups, and forty males and forty-four females who declined to participate in such groups. Multivariate analysis showed participatory status to be significant beyond the .01 level, with participants higher on the major Inner-Directed (I) and Time Competence (TC) scales. The participating female group was higher than all other groups on nine of the ten POI subscales, indicating that females in particular seeking encounter group experience may be more self-actualizing. Noll and Watkins suggest that group workers wishing to attend to sex differences of participants may find males to be worse off initially and perhaps more difficult to work with. Sheridan and Shack (1970) found that among college students enrolled in a Personality-Problems-and-Mental-Health course, those volunteering for a sensitivity-training experience—as contrasted with those not volunteering—scored significantly higher on only one POI subscale: Self-Acceptance. Gilligan (1973) compared fifty-three volunteer college students selecting sensitivity training with a sample of fifty-six nonselectors. Those selecting the training were significantly higher on the Inner-Directed scale and the Existentiality, Spontaneity, and Capacity for Intimate Contact subscales.

The initial level of POI scores based on the many other encounter group studies considered below gives further support to the notion that the more-actualizing person, rather than the "disturbed" individual, is likely to seek encounter.

Studies of Change Following Encounter

A number of studies have demonstrated the sensitivity of the POI in measuring changes in self-actualizing following encounter group experience. A summary of the results of the major studies is presented in Table 3.

In an extensive study of the effects of nonprofessionally led encounter groups with university and community volunteers, Bebout and Gordon (1972) reported the results of pre- and post-encounter group experience. The sample for which POI analyses were reported involved seventy males and sixty-five females. Pre- to post-test changes were analyzed separately for the sexes and significant increases were obtained for the major Inner-Directed scale as well as for the Existentiality (males only), Feeling Reactivity, Spontaneity, Acceptance of Aggression, and Capacity for Intimate Contact subscales. Although the analysis suffers from lack of a control sample, the increases are in line with several other studies employing smaller samples and incorporating control samples in their design.

To examine the effects of a program of transcendental meditation on self-actualizing as measured by the POI, Seeman, Nidich, and Banta (1972) administered the POI to an experimental group of twenty college students—and a control group of twenty—prior to initiation of the program and two months following completion of the program. The mean difference for the experimental group on the Inner/Other support dimension was significantly higher than for the control group at the .02 confidence level. Significant mean changes in the positive direction were obtained for the experimental group on the major Inner-Directed scale and subscales of Self-Actualizing Value, Spontaneity, Acceptance of Aggression, and Capacity for Intimate Contact. No pre- to post-test changes were significant for the control group.

In a replication of the above study, Nidich, Seeman, and Dreskin (1973) reported significant increases on the major Inner-Directed and Time Competence scales with significant differences on eight of the ten subscales. None of the changes for a control sample reached significance. Profiles for the pre- and post-test administrations are presented in Figure 7 as an il-

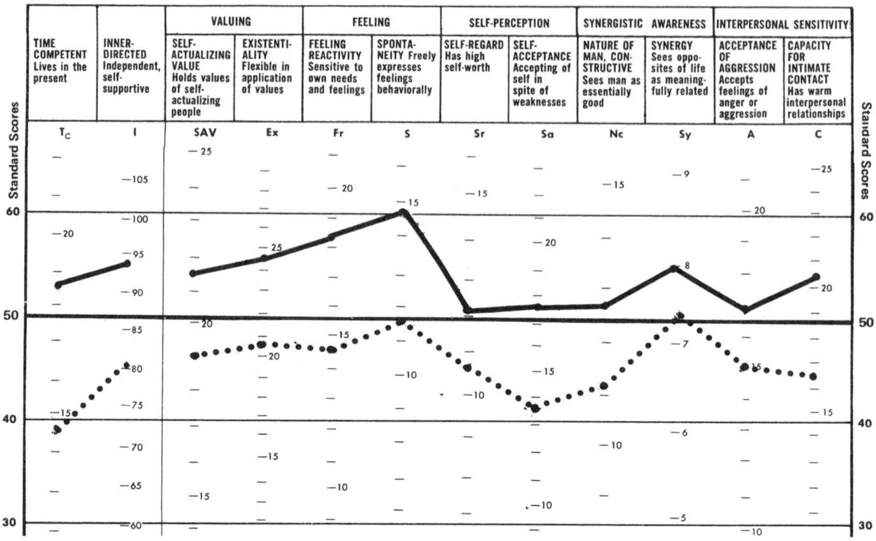

	Tc	I	SAV	Ex	Fr	S	Sr	Sa	Nc	Sy	A	C
Post-Test (—) (N=9)												
m	18.7	94.6	21.7	24.8	18.1	14.6	12.1	17.8	12.6	8.0	17.0	20.3
σ	3.3	12.6	2.9	4.8	2.3	2.1	3.0	3.6	2.4	.9	3.7	4.2
Pre-Test (---) (N=9)												
m	14.7	80.8	19.0	20.7	14.6	11.7	10.7	13.8	11.2	7.3	15.0	16.7
σ	3.3	10.4	3.3	4.8	3.3	2.6	1.4	2.9	2.2	1.2	2.7	4.3

From Nidich, Seeman and Dreskin (1973).

Figure 7. POI Profiles for Pre- and Post-Test Administrations to a Sample of Students in Transcendental Meditation.

lustration ot the effects of group participation for those in the transcendental meditation sample.

Trueblood and McHolland (1971) have reported on the effects of the "human potential" group process in helping students to become more self-actualizing. The POI was administered twice to two groups of junior-college students, one consisting of thirty-three students enrolled in a fourteen week human potential seminar and the other a control sample of sixty-two students. Analysis of the results showed that the number of students in the experimental group who changed in a positive direction was significantly higher than in the control group. In the experimental group, significant changes between pre- and post-treatment administration were found on the major scale of Inner-Directed and on subscales of Self-Actualizing Value, Existentiality, Self-Regard, and Nature of Man-Constructive. In a study using pre- and post-treatment POI administrations with a small college sample (N = 7 experimental, 7 control) in a fifteen-hour marathon group experience, Young and Jacobson (1970) found significant increase on only one subscale, the Self-Actualizing Value scale.

Guinan and Foulds (1970) report changes on POI scale scores following a marathon group experience. The study was designed to investigate such changes as might occur among a group of relatively "normal" college students following a voluntary, thirty-hour weekend marathon experience. Results were compared with those obtained from a selected control sample volunteering to be in "an experiment." Analysis of the data disclosed that mean POI scores for the experimental marathon group changed significantly in a positive direction for the major Inner-Directed scale as well as for six of the subscales: Existentiality, Feeling Reactivity, Spontaneity, Self-Acceptance, Acceptance of Aggression, and Capacity for Intimate Contact. No changes for the control group reached significance. Use of a control group and the highly significant results obtained comparing group pre- and post-experimental scores are important aspects of this study.

In two related studies, Foulds (1970, 1971) reported similar changes in POI scores following an eight or nine-week growth group experience in which groups met for one four to four-and-one-half hour period per week.

Findings of the Guinan and Foulds (1970) study were challenged by Marks, Conry, and Foster (1973) on the basis of shortcomings in the design of the study. In a subsequent study, very carefully designed to meet these criticisms, Foulds and Hannigan (in press) obtained much the same results as in their earlier study. Volunteer subjects were randomly assigned to experimental and control groups. Significantly greater increases in measures of self-actualizing were obtained for those in the encounter experience, as contrasted with a control group, in terms of the major POI Inner-Directed scale and eight of the ten POI subscales. The only subscales failing to reach significance were the Nature of Man and Synergy scales. An important facet of this study was the inclusion of a six-month follow-up administration of the POI. Rather than showing longer-term regression effects, the six month follow-up revealed significant positive gains in overall level of self-actualizing when compared with levels achieved at the end of the marathon group. Results of this study are illustrated in Figure 8.

In a similarly designed study by Treppa and Fricke (1972) further evidence, bearing especially upon the issue of the comparative effects of control versus marathon group experience on POI scores, has been presented. The POI, along with other personality inventories, was administered prior to and following a weekend marathon group experience and again as a six week follow-up. Both experimental and control groups, with sample sizes of eleven each, showed significant positive changes on post-test and follow-up scores. Although changes from pre-test to post-test reached significance (beyond the .05 confidence level) for the two major scales and five of the subscales in the experimental group, as compared with only one major and one subscale in the subscale in the control group, the interaction effect between groups and test condition reached significance for only the POI subscale of Spontaneity. Changes from pre-test to post-test were all in the positive direction in the experimental group while, in the control group, four of the twelve changes were in the negative direction. The authors concluded that the data from their study failed to adequately demonstrate the positive effects of the marathon group experience.

A study reported by the Counseling Center Staff, University of Massachusetts (1972), and employing the POI in evaluating the effects of

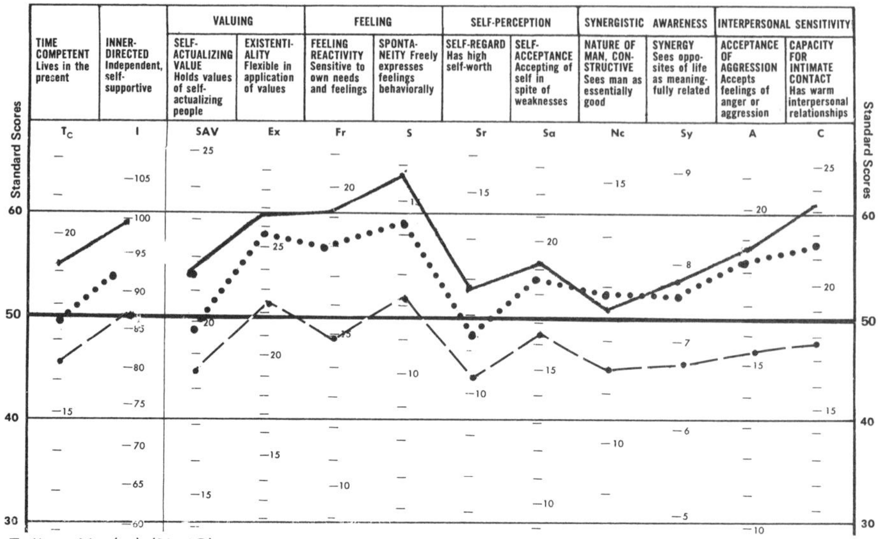

	Tc	I	SAV	Ex	Fr	S	Sr	Sa	Nc	Sy	A	C
Follow-Up (—) (N=18)												
m	19.2	99.9	21.3	26.8	19.2	15.7	12.7	19.1	12.5	7.7	18.8	23.1
σ	2.9	7.9	2.4	2.2	2.7	2.2	2.2	3.3	1.7	1.0	2.7	2.2
Post-Test (···) (N=18)												
m	17.4	94.7	19.8	25.6	18.0	14.3	11.5	18.8	12.7	7.5	18.4	21.3
σ	3.2	10.9	3.6	3.0	3.2	2.3	3.2	3.1	2.0	1.1	2.9	2.8
Pre-Test (---) (N=18)												
m	16.3	85.4	18.5	22.4	14.9	12.1	10.3	16.2	11.4	6.7	15.4	17.8
σ	3.9	11.9	3.9	3.7	3.6	3.0	3.1	3.9	2.7	1.4	3.0	3.0

From Foulds and Hannigan (in press)

Figure 8. POI Profiles for Pre-Test, Post-Test and Follow-Up Administrations to a Sample in a Marathon Group Experience.

group participation, failed to demonstrate positive results. Forty-two volunteer college students participating in one of three types of short duration (ten-hour participation) sensitivity groups were compared with six control students recruited from a class. Although significant increases on POI scales were observed in all three treatment groups, the increases registered among the six students in the control group were such that, when submitted to multiple discriminant analysis, results failed to support the hypothesis that group participation would produce greater change in self-actualizing. As the authors note in the extended report, the control subjects were non-participants who had not sought a sensitivity group experience. Other limitations noted by the authors concerned the short amount of time spent in group meetings and the high within-group variability obtained on post-test.

Kimball and Gelso (1974) contrasted the results of the Treppa and Fricke and University of Massachusetts studies with three others—Foulds (1971), Guinan and Foulds (1970), and Young and Jacobson (1970)—in which positive results were obtained. Their analysis yielded two salient factors differentiating studies with positive results from those with negative results:

the number of group leaders and the total amount of meeting time. With regard to number of leaders, the Treppa and Fricke (1972) study used only one facilitator while, of those obtaining positive results, two used two leaders each and the third a highly experienced facilitator. With regard to meeting time, the studies that obtained positive results employed a minimum of fifteen hours of group time, as contrasted with ten hours and an unspecified amount of time in those obtaining negative results.

In their own study employing fourteen experiemental and fourteen control subjects in an eighteen-hour weekend marathon experience, Kimball and Gelso (1974) obtained significant results on the major Inner-Directed scale and four subscales: Spontaneity, Self-Regard, Self-Acceptance, and Synergy.

Longer-Term Effects of Encounter

A question frequently asked of those who espouse the encounter group experience is whether the effects are merely transitory or are of a more permanent nature. Several studies have evaluated the level of self-actualizing as measured by the POI over periods of from six to nine weeks and up to one year following the encounter group experience. One important study, that of Foulds and Hannigan (in press, a) has already been discussed above and the results presented in Figure 8.

Alperson, Alperson, and Levine (1971) examined the effect of a marathon encounter group experience on POI scores among high-school students. Thirty-two volunteer students were unsystematically assigned to a control (no marathon treatment) or experimental (marathon treatment) group and completed the POI as a pre-treatment and post-treatment measure. Increases in POI scores for the experimental group reached significance for the two major scales of Time Competence and Inner-Directed and for the subscales of Existentiality, Self-Regard, Self-Acceptance, and Acceptance of Aggression. The major scales were not significantly different for the control group and only one subscale, Feeling Reactivity, showed a significant increase at the .05 level. The authors conclude that marathon encounters can contribute to growth in terms of these POI scales.

In examining the effectiveness of a human relations training program among rural high-school teachers, Banmen and Capelle (1972) used the POI to measure pre- to post-test changes in a sample of thirty-two educators volunteering for a three-and-one- half day program. Gains following the program (four days following the program) were significant for the major Inner-Directed scale and for five subscales: Existentiality, Feeling Reactivity, Self-Acceptance, Acceptance of Aggression, and Capacity for Intimate Contact. As a part of the design of this study, participants were readministered the POI three months following the program. In the follow-up scores, all of the above scales reached significance and, in addition, the Spontaneity subscale reached significance at the .05 level. None of the differences between post-test and follow-up measures reached significance. Thus, changes immediately following the program were consistent with

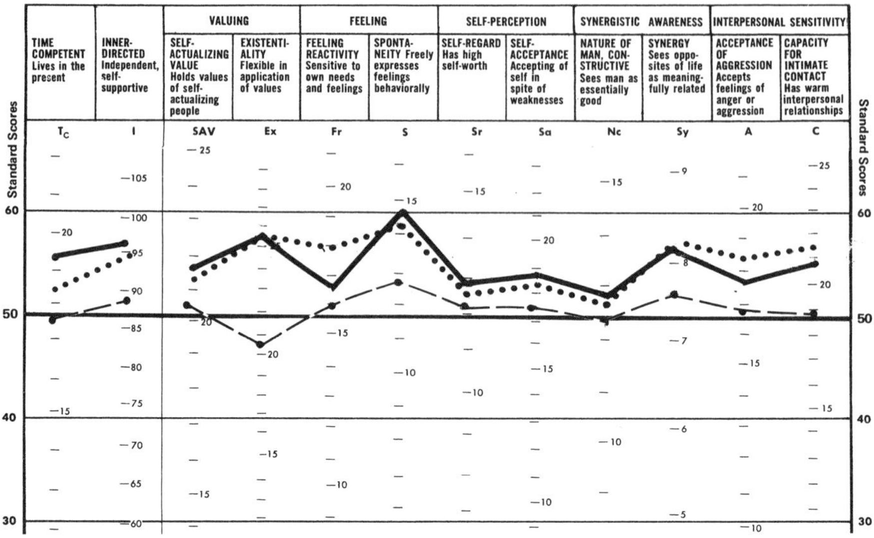

	Tc	I	SAV	Ex	Fr	S	Sr	Sa	Nc	Sy	A	C
Follow-Up (—) (N=36)												
m	19.3	95.4	21.4	25.1	16.9	14.7	12.9	18.6	12.7	8.1	17.8	20.9
Post-Test (···) (N=36)												
m	18.5	94.8	21.1	25.1	18.0	14.1	12.6	18.1	12.5	8.1	18.3	21.1
Pre-Test (- - -) (N=36)												
m	17.8	88.1	20.4	20.5	16.0	12.9	12.4	17.4	12.2	7.6	16.8	18.9

From Reddy (1973)

Figure 9. POI Profiles for Pre-Test, Post-Test, and Follow-Up Administrations to a Sample of YMCA Administrators.

numerous other studies available and were also maintained over a three-month period.

Investigating the longer-term effects of a ten-day sensitivity training laboratory, Reddy (1973) administered the POI prior to the first group meeting, prior to the last group meeting, and one year from the close of the laboratory. Profiles based on mean POI scores are presented in Figure 9. Interaction effects over time were significant for the major POI scales of Time Competence and Inner-Directed as well as for seven of the ten sub-scales. Results were interpreted as demonstrating that sensitivity training group participants exhibited changes in measures of self-actualizing and that these changes were maintained or continued over time. The results further suggested that participants exhibited change at different rates and at different times. While some participants showed substantial gains in self-actualizing at the close of the laboratory, others exhibited major gains after returning to their usual environment. Further analysis showed that this differential rate was related to level of anxiety of the participants as measured by the *Multiple Affect Adjective Check Test* (Zuckerman & Lubin, 1965). Correlations between POI changes and the measure of anxiety suggested that particpants who experienced higher levels of anxiety during the laboratory did not exhibit changes on the POI at the close of the laboratory.

Intellectualized versus Honestly Felt Expression

Another issue involves the question of whether measured changes merely reflect an intellectualized response. Ample evidence has accumulated to demonstrate the effects of the encounter group experience in producing significant self-reported changes toward self-actualizing. In terms of the three aspects or expressions of being—*thinking, feeling,* and *bodily expression*—presented by Shostrom, Knapp, and Knapp (1976), such changes may primarily reflect growth at the thinking, or intellectualized, level. It might be asked to what extent these may be reflected in changes in the feeling and bodily expression levels of this continuum. While very little evidence has been presented to date on this topic, a few studies are pertinent.

In their study of the effects of sensitivity training among university students, Culbert, Clark, and Bobele (1968) administered the POI before and after a series of two-hour sensitivity training meetings. When divided into initially "actualizing" and "normal" groups, those with initially high POI scores showed significant increases on the major Inner-Directed scale and on the subscales of Spontaneity, Synergy, and Capacity for Intimate Contact. Of particular interest for the present discussion are correlations between the POI and a measure of self-aware verbal behavior. While the POI is a measure of self-percepts at the thinking level, self-aware verbal behavior was assumed to be a measure of self-actualizing behavior itself. In this part of the study, no significant relationships were obtained. Thus, in this study, although an initially low actualizing sample showed significant POI score changes (thinking level), these changes were not reflected in increased self-aware verbal behavior (bodily expression level).

In another study related to this issue, Walton (1973) administered the POI to groups of college students enrolled in a seminar in humanistic psychology. Those in the two experimental groups received didactic content instruction as well as ten to fourteen one-hour-long personal growth group sessions. Students in a control group received instruction concerning counseling concepts, including the concepts and counseling procedures for furthering self-actualizing. However, no systematic training experience was provided. Comparisons of pre-test to post-test changes on the POI showed that students in both groups receiving the training experience increased on the major Inner-Directed scale. Changes on this scale for the control group receiving instruction only did not reach significance. Subscale changes reaching significance for the experimental groups were Existentiality, Spontaneity, Self-Acceptance, and Capacity for Intimate Contact. For the control group, taught by didactic procedures, only the Nature of Man scale showed significant increase. Findings were interpreted as supporting the hypothesis that personal growth groups are productive of psychological growth as defined by the POI.

Studies involving attempts to "fake" POI results are of some relevance to this topic. It has been shown that, generally, instructions to fake, or make a good impression, on the POI actually result in profiles characteristic of less self-actualized individuals. However, in their previously described study of the faking of POI responses, Braun and La Faro (1969) included two experimental groups that received discussion of the concept of self-actualizing intervening between standard and faked administrations. Mean scores for the major Inner-Directed scale significantly increased in one group but not in the other. Results of their study suggested that "the inventory shows an unexpected resistance to faking" but that with specific knowledge about the inventory and the concepts measured, persons can improve their POI scores under certain circumstances. These studies are discussed in greater detail in Chapter 3.

In a series of studies in which college students were presented either information about the concept of self-actualizing, information about more conventional social adjustment, or no information, Warehime, Routh, and Foulds (1974) found that those receiving information about actualizing were able to increase their scores on the POI when asked to use this information. However, when asked to respond honestly, their scores were unaffected by knowledge about self-actualizing. The authors concluded that the Inner-Directed scale is more resistant to faking than many other self-report inventories and that the POI is "remarkably unsusceptible to dissimulation."

Although the evidence is as yet sketchy in this area, it appears that the encounter group experience does produce POI changes beyond those produced by intellectualized, didactic instruction.

Comparison of Encounter Training Techniques

A question of broad implication, but one which barely has been researched, involves comparisons between different encounter experience techniques. Using samples of thirty-three in an experimental "creative risk taking" training group and thirty-eight in a standard sensitivity training control group, Byrd (1967) compared the relative effectiveness of sensitivity training procedure with other procedures collectively designated as "creative risk taking" among church professionals. Significantly greater increases were obtained for the experimental group on five POI scales (Inner-Directed, Self-Actualizing Values, Spontaneity, Nature of Man-Constructive, and Acceptance of Aggression), thus suggesting the possible superiority of the experimental techniques under the circumstances of this study.

Summary

A consistent pattern of increased self-actualizing scores following group training programs emerges from examination of studies on this topic. Although most of the studies to date have employed very small samples, significant differences have been obtained in most instances between pre- and post-treatment administrations of the POI and, in aggregate, present a very uniform picture of increased self-actualizing as measured by the POI.

Although the composition of the samples and nature of the treatment experience varies greatly among the studies, a fairly consistent picture emerges when viewed in terms of the summary Table 3 on page 32. The overwhelming preponderance of significant increases in POI scores occurred within the experimental groups, with only a few significant increases occurring in control samples. Of the nine studies considered in which treatment results were compared with a control sample not involved in encounter training, fifty-six significant increases were observed in the experimental group, while only three increases reached significance in the control samples. All studies except one (eight out of nine) reported significant increases on the major Inner-Directed scale. In terms of subscale interpretation of this demonstrated increase in inner-support, the greatest number of studies (eight) demonstrated increases in Spontaneity. Other frequently observed increases were in Existentiality, Acceptance of Aggression, and Capacity for Intimate Contact scales, each showing increases in six of the ten studies. Scales of Self-Actualizing Values and Self-Acceptance each demonstrated increases in five of the ten studies. Increases in other scales reached significance in less than half of the studies and thus may be considered to be relatively less subject to change under the conditions imposed and the techniques generally employed in group experiences.

EMPIRICAL VERIFICATION OF THEORETICAL CONSTRUCTS OF SELF-ACTUALIZING

It would appear natural that the POI would be the chosen instrument for researchers interested in empirical investigations of humanist concepts of self-actualizing. Developed in consultation with Abraham Maslow, the POI covers many of the concepts encompassed in his theory of the self-actualizing person. As Maslow noted about the POI in his last published book (1971), "[The POI] correlates well with external variables of various kinds, and keeps on accumulating additional correlational meanings. As a result, I feel heuristically justified in *starting* with my 'determined naiveté.' Most of what I was able to see intuitively, directly, personally, is being confirmed now with numbers, tables and curves" (p. 28).

Among the early applications of the POI bearing on confirmation of Maslow's theory was a study by the present author (Knapp, 1965) in which self-actualizing as measured by the POI was shown to be negatively related to the concept of neuroticism as measured by the *Eysenck Personality Inventory* (Eysenck & Eysenck, 1963). When divided, on the basis of EPI scores, into samples of comparatively "neurotic" and "emotionally stable" college students, the more emotionally stable were higher on all POI scales, as illustrated in Figure 10. As noted by Hilgard and Atkinson (1967) these results "would support Maslow's contention that he was describing mentally healthy people" (p. 160). A number of subsequent studies have related POI scores to concepts of adjustment represented in other instruments. Examples are (1) the data of Shostrom and Knapp (1966), described earlier, in which the POI was shown to be negatively related to measures of pathology

TABLE 3

Significant Pre to Post Increases for POI Scales in Major Encounter Group Studies

POI Scales		Studies With Control Group									Without Control				
	Study	Alperson, Alperson & Levine (1971)	Byrd (1967)	Foulds & Hannigan (in press)	Guinan & Foulds (1970)	Kimball & Gelso (1974)	Seeman, Nidick & Banta (1972)	Treppa & Fricke (1972)	Walton (1973)	Young & Jacobson (1970)	Banmen & Capelle (1972)	Bebout & Gordon (1972)	Culbert, Clark & Bobele (1968)	Knapp & Fitzgerald (1973)	Reddy (1973)
		Experimental Group													
Time Competence	(TC)	**		**				*							**
Inner-Directed	(I)	**	*	**	**	**	**	*	**		**	**	**	**	**
Self-Actualizing Value	(SAV)	*	*	**			*			**					*
Existentiality	(Ex)	**		**	**			**	*		**	**			**
Feeling Reactivity	(Fr)	*		**	**						**	*		**	**
Spontaneity	(S)	*	**	**	**	**	**	*	**			**	*	**	**
Self-Regard	(Sr)	**		**		**	**	*						**	
Self-Acceptance	(Sa)	**		**	**	*		**	*		**				**
Nature of Man (Constructive)	(Nc)		*												
Synergy	(Sy)	*				*							*		*
Acceptance of Aggression	(A)	*	**	**	*		**	*			**	**		**	
Capacity for Intimate Contact	(C)	*		**	**		*				**	**	*		**
		Control Group													
Time Competence	(TC)														
Inner-Directed	(I)							*							
Self-Actualizing Value	(SAV)														
Existentiality	(Ex)														
Feeling Reactivity	(Fr)	*													
Spontaneity	(S)														
Self-Regard	(Sr)														
Self-Acceptance	(Sa)														
Nature of Man (Constructive)	(Nc)							**		**					
Synergy	(Sy)														
Acceptance of Aggression	(A)														
Capacity for Intimate Contact	(C)														

*Significant at the .05 confidence level.

**Significant at the .01 confidence level

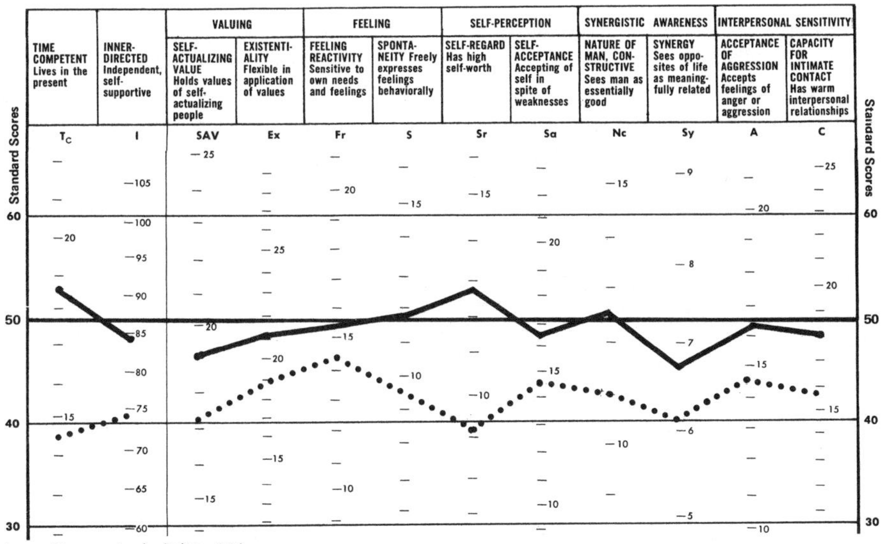

Low Neurotic (—) (N=38)

	Tc	I	SAV	Ex	Fr	S	Sr	Sa	Nc	Sy	A	C
m	18.2	84.1	19.0	21.1	15.3	11.7	12.8	16.5	12.5	6.8	16.2	18.0
σ	2.2	8.3	2.8	3.1	2.7	2.3	1.6	2.9	1.6	1.1	3.3	3.2

High Neurotic (- - -) (N=38)

	Tc	I	SAV	Ex	Fr	S	Sr	Sa	Nc	Sy	A	C
m	14.4	74.0	17.1	19.0	14.2	9.2	9.3	14.7	11.0	6.1	14.9	15.9
σ	2.8	9.3	2.6	3.7	2.9	2.2	2.3	3.8	1.9	1.3	3.1	3.5

From Knapp (1965)

Figure 10. POI Profiles for a "High" Neurotic and a "Low" Neurotic College Sample.

obtained from the MMPI; (2) the evidence, presented by Knapp and Comrey (1973), of a high relationship between a factorial measure of emotional stability obtained from the *Comrey Personality Scales* (CPS; Comrey, 1970) and self-actualizing as measured by the POI; and (3) the study by Mattocks and Jew (1974) in which the PoI was shown to be positively related to the concept of the "well-adjusted person" as defined by the Dymond (1954) Q-Sort Adjustment Scale.

Verification of hypotheses generated from Maslow's theory of self-actualization provided the basis of a study by Hekmat and Theiss (1971). Maslow's maxim of the self-actualizing individual's "resistance to enculturation" was studied through a social-conditioning technique. The hypothesis was that persons with low scores would respond more to reflection of feeling as a reinforcer for affective self-disclosures than would those with moderate or high scores. The POI was administered to sixty subjects, who were assigned on the basis of their scores to one of four groups: high self-actualizing, moderate self-actualizing, low self-actualizing, and control. Conditioning consisted of reflective statements by the experimenter to every self-disclosure comment made by each subject during interviews. The results indicated that, prior to conditioning, the high-self-actualizing individuals displayed a significantly higher rate of affective self-disclosures than did the moderate- or low-self-actualizing group. During conditioning, however, the high-self-actualizing individuals showed a significantly lower degree of responsiveness to social reinforcement when compared to the low- and moderate-self-actualizers. Thus, analysis of adjusted scores indicated that the low-self-actualizing group had the highest rate of conditioning. The high-self-actualizing individuals showed a nonsignificant gain in rate of affective self-disclosures during conditioning. Results were interpreted as providing empirical support for Maslow's assertion that high-self-actualizing individuals are "resistant to enculturation."

As Hekmat and Theiss (1971) note, a goal of psychotherapy may be to help the client achieve "intrinsic learning (becoming)" through reflection. As they further note, their results suggest that "as an individual moves toward self-actualization, the locus of effective reinforcement may move from the external to the internal source and the traditional therapeutic technique thus becomes less effective" (p. 105). Hekmat and Theiss further speculate that the highly self-actualizing individual responds more to the therapist as a model rather than as a dispenser of reinforcement. They further suggest that therapists with high levels of genuineness, authenticity, and self-disclosure may achieve the most effective behavior modification with high-self-actualizing clients. These findings add significantly to previous findings concerning the relationship of self-actualization to counseling effectiveness.

Maslow's (1970) conjecture that conformity would be negatively related to self-actualizing received experimental support from a study reported by Crosson and Schwendiman (1972). POI Inner-Directed scale scores were used as the measure of self-actualizing, and conformity was measured under social pressure by a Crutchfield apparatus with perceptual-discrimination judgments consisting of matching the lengths of lines and choosing the largest relative area of geometrical figures. Thus, as the authors note, design of the study extends the construct validity of the POI to objective, behavioral predictions and adds to the number of verifications of the nomological network extending from the self-actualizing model. Conformity behavior in a group setting is of theoretical moment to the concept of self-actualizing. Maslow has described the actualizing person as one who would feel no constraint to yield to social influences. This independence from social pressures should hold for pressure to conform to the expectations of the group and for the use of others' responses as information. Thus it was hypothesized that relatively self-actualizing individuals would exhibit independent behavior in a conformity situation. The obtained correlation of -.28 between the Inner-Directed scale scores and the conformity behavioral score was significant beyond the .025 confidence level and was accepted as supporting the hypothesis of a negative relationship between self-actualizing and conformity. Although significant, the obtained correlation is low, which may be due to restriction in range of the POI scores. Subjects in this study were introductory psychology students among whom representation of comparatively more self-actualizing individuals is usually curtailed, a fact further supported in this study by the observation that the distribution of the Inner-Directed scores had a slight positive skewness, with most subjects falling in the nonactualizing range.

In a related study, Zimmerman, Smith, and Pedersen (1970) found low but generally positive correlations between a measure of conformity and POI scales in each of three treatment groups ranging in size from thirty-five to forty-six. One correlation, that between Spontaneity scale scores and conformity behavior reached significance at the .05 confidence level (r=.27). Due to the inconsistent pattern of correlations in the three treatment groups, no overall conclusion could be reached concerning the relationship of POI scales to conformity behavior. Doyle (1975), in a sample of 150 subjects, reported that nine of the twelve POI scales were significantly correlated with the field-independent perceptual style as measured by Witkin's Rod-and-frame Test.

Findings from investigations among college-student samples are, in fact, consistent with the observation made by Maslow (1970), who, in searching a college campus for self-actualized subjects, stated, "I had to conclude that self-actualization of the sort I had found in my older subjects perhaps was not possible in our society for young, developing people" (p. 150). In comparison to adult samples, high-school and early college mean scores fall generally in a T-score range of 40 to 45. Profiles for representative samples of high-school students and entering college freshmen are presented in Figure 11.

Results from a number of studies reported in the section on Underachievement (p. 18) have been interpreted as providing support for the conceptualization of self-actualizing in terms of an educational model of personal development. For example, Leib and Snyder's (1967) interpretation of the beneficial effect upon both achievement and self-actualizing of underachievers supports Maslow's concept of the development of self-actualization by providing the special attention that met needs of belongingness, love, and esteem, releasing these individuals for further personal development. Similarly, Pearson (1966) interpreted the increases in self-actualizing resulting from a group-directed form of guidance as reflecting an increased self-acceptance generated by the confidence placed in students' ability to find effective solutions to problems. Such process, when viewed as part of the psychological "chain reaction" described by Rogers (1951, pp. 481-533) in his theory of personality and behavior, gives theoretical credence to the application of the actualizing model in educational situations.

Relationship to Other Theoretical Systems

Shostrom, through logical analysis, has related his system of Actualizing Therapy (Shostrom, Knapp, & Knapp, 1976) to the therapeutic systems of Rogers, Ellis, and Perls. Empirical studies recently reported have also clarified the relationships between concepts defining these approaches.

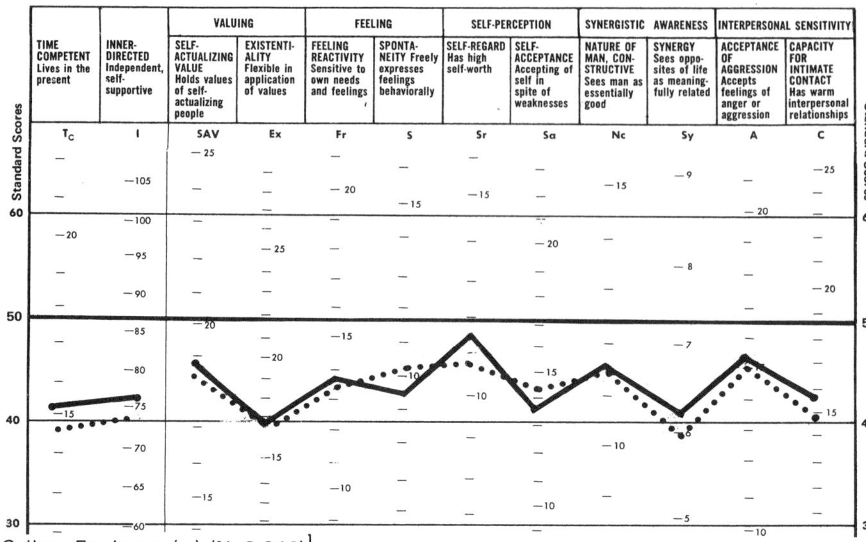

College Freshmen (—) (N=2,046)[1]

	Tc	I	SAV	Ex	Fr	S	Sr	Sa	Nc	Sy	A	C
m	15.1	75.6	18.8	16.7	13.8	9.7	11.5	13.7	11.6	6.3	15.1	15.6
σ	2.9	8.9	2.6	4.4	2.9	2.2	2.2	3.1	2.0	1.4	3.0	3.4

High School Students (- - -) (N=412)[2]

	Tc	I	SAV	Ex	Fr	S	Sr	Sa	Nc	Sy	A	C
m	14.8	74.8	18.2	16.7	13.4	10.2	10.9	14.1	11.5	6.0	15.0	14.9
σ	2.9	8.5	2.7	3.8	2.9	2.6	2.2	3.0	1.9	1.3	2.9	3.6

[1] Based on data presented by Daryl D. Jenkins.

[2] Based on data reported by William R. Weir.

Figure 11. POI Profiles for an Entering College Freshman Sample and a High School Sample.

Morris (1974) used the POI and the Adult Irrational Ideas Inventory with a prisoner sample to investigate the relationship between the underlying constructs of the Self Theory of Carl Rogers and the Rational-Emotive Theory advanced by Albert Ellis. As hypothesized, the measure of irrationality was consistently and negatively correlated with the POI. The two major POI scales and six of the ten subscales were significantly correlated with a total Irrational Ideas score.

Phillips, Watkins, and Noll (1974) empirically contrasted the self-actualizing theory as measured by the POI with the self-transcendence theory proposed by Frankl (1966) and as measured by the Purpose in Life Test (Crumbaugh & Maholick, 1969). Correlations against POI scales were generally low, including a nonsignificant correlation of .13 against the major Inner-Directed scale. However, correlations reached significance against three POI scales: Time Competence (*r*=.39), Self-Actualizing Value (*r*=.41), and Self-Regard (*r*=.46). Thus, although measuring different aspects of personal growth, the concepts measured by the Purpose in Life Test more closely parallel the measures of emotional stability and trust reflected in POI Self-Regard and Nature of Man scales. The relationship of POI constructs to factorial theories of personality is presented in the section on Correlational Studies.

Inner- versus Other-Directedness: Locus of Control and Self-Actualizing

Locus of control is hypothesized to be a personality dimension referring to the way an individual characteristically perceives himself in interaction with the environment. Persons with an *internal* orientation perceive themselves as having personal control over their reinforcements as a consequence of their behavior. Those with an *external* orientation perceive reinforcements as being independent of their behavior and beyond their personal control.

Rotter (1966) has hypothesized a positive relationship between perceived locus of control and personal adjustment. From this theory, persons who view positive reinforcements as contingent upon their own behavior (internals) are better adjusted than those who see reinforcements as determined by chance, fate, or powerful others (externals). Internals depict themselves as active, striving, achieving, powerful, independent, and effective. Internality has been found to be associated with insight, constructive responses to frustration, and efforts to better one's life circumstances, while externality has been associated with anxiety, neuroticism, death anxiety, suicide, accident proneness, and pathology.

In a study to determine the relationship of self-actualizing to locus of control, Wareheim and Foulds (1971) found a hypothesized significant relationship between POI measures of Inner-Directed support (I scale scores) and internal locus of control measured by the Rotter IE scale. Correlations of greatest magnitude were against POI scales of Self-Regard (r = -.33), Time Competence (r = -.32), and Nature of Man (r = -.27) for a sample of fifty-five female college students. Such a relationship was not found for a similar sample of fifty-five males.

In an unpublished study conducted by Lovekin (1972) the POI and the IE scale were admininstered to participants in a five-day encounter group human relations institute. Although, as hypothesized, increases on the POI were significant for the major POI Inner-Directed scale and nine of the subscales, such increases were not significantly greater for those persons whose locus of control was identified as internal as contrasted with the externals. Other investigations (Collins, Martin, Ashmore, & Ross, in press) have found the POI Inner/Other support scale to fit consistently with dimensional analysis.

Relationships in these studies are consistent with, and amplify, the results of an important study by Margulies (1969) in which higher levels of self-actualizing were found to be associated with intrinsic, as contrasted with extrinsic, work values. More information will be given about the implications of POI research to organizational structure in the section on Industry (p. 42).

RESULTS FROM POPULATIONS OF SPECIAL INTEREST

Education

Self-actualizing theory, as it relates to education, might be interpreted to imply that the goals of the curriculum should be the facilitation of the natural strivings of each student toward his or her highest potential level of uniqueness, autonomy, and self-fulfillment.

Maslow (1971) has stated that the chief goals of the ideal college "would be the *discovery of identity*, and with it, the *discovery of vocation*" (p. 183). Schools would thus provide a setting for self-discovery, for finding out real desires and characteristics, and for determining a lifestyle to express these. The schools would then be helping students to look within themselves, thus providing them with the self-knowledge from which a set of values might be derived.

Maslow (1971) brings attention to the ways in which the school curriculum regiments, constricts, and molds—crushing the self-discovery, creativity, and peak experiences that ultimately lead to greater self-actualizing. In this view, too much of the education system is devoted to the passing on of knowledge through coverage of a given subject matter in a given period of time. It is the minority of humanistically oriented educators—having as their goal the creation of "better," self-actualizing and self-transcendent human beings—about whose endeavors the present treatise is concerned.

Perhaps the major innovative change in the public-school curriculum to which the POI has been applied is in the evaluation of recently introduced programs of group experience techniques. Several studies at the high-school and college levels have attempted to assess the effects of such experience in terms of the increased self-actualizing of participants. Studies by Alperson, Alperson, and Levine (1971) and Banmen and Capelle (1972) with high-school students and by Foulds and Hannigan (in press) and Seeman, Nidich, Banta (1972) with college students (presented in Chapter 2 under *Evaluation of Effects of Encounter Group Experience*) illustrate the use of the POI in evaluation of such experience.

A number of additional studies involving use of the POI carry implications for the implementation of a curriculum based on self-actualizing theory. These studies may generally be classified in two broad areas: those relating to measurement of student effectiveness and those relating to teacher effectiveness.

Actualizing implies personal growth and emotional maturation—both aspects of the learning process. Certainly, within the school and college setting, the opportunity should exist for the consistent stimulation of affective growth, both for the child/adolescent subculture and for those who participate in the education of youth. As the above studies have indicated, certain educational techniques are now being employed to promote such augmentation: the growth group experience and the impact of the teacher (as shown by Coble, 1973) or counselor (as shown by Weinrach, 1972) who is demonstrably actualizing. Hopefully, such teachers and counselors further serve as a positive social model. The school environment and its routine constitute a formal lifestyle in which guided social interaction and the cognitive inculcation of knowledge go hand in hand. As Brown (1971) points out in his *Introduction to Confluent Education*, "A healthy society ... allows its members to grow toward authenticity, communication, and productivity. It makes available a continuing choice between the tranquillity of reflection and the excitement and gratification of individual and group creative endeavor no matter what the focus of creativity" (p. 9). Significantly, it is this same creativity that the POI—in the hands of the researcher Damm (1970)—was able to demonstrate as being related to self-actualization.

Progress is typically incremental, and the assessment of degrees of progress requires an instrument sensitive to the broad spectrum of affective growth. The image of the educational process is changing, and the POI is providing replicable data on the magnitude and direction of the change. Hopefully, application of results from its use are thereby contributing to a more emotionally stimulating school setting.

Student Effectiveness

In studying the relative contributions of creativity and intelligence to self-actualizing, Damm (1970) analyzed results from the Inner-Directed scale of the POI, an overall estimate of intelligence, and measures of the ability to think creatively. Correlation between the POI and the measure of creativity, although of a low magnitude (r = .19), was significant—supporting the hypothesis of a positive relationship between self-actualizing and creativity. To investigate the hypothesis that greatest levels of self-actualizing would be achieved when both creative and intellectual abilities are maximized, the sample was divided into four independent groups: high-intelligence/high-creativity, high-intelligence/low-creativity, low-intelligence/high-creativity, and low-intelligence/low-creativity. Analysis of the data indicated significant interaction and showed that the group of students who had obtained high scores on *both* intelligence and creativity were more self-actualizing than those who had obtained a high score *only* on intelligence or *only* on creativity. Furthermore, the high-intelligence/high-creativity group was more self-actualizing than the low-intelligence/low-creativity group, as predicted. Damm concluded that if education has as its goal the productive self-fulfillment of every student, the curriculum should encourage a development of both intellectual and creative abilities, rather than a concentration on one to the exclusion of the other.

In studying self-actualizing among extremely superior college students, McClain and Andrews (1972) found that only the Self-Regard subscale of the POI differentiated a sample of intellectually gifted students selected for scholarships from an unselected sample of college seniors.

Related studies concerned with effects of counseling techniques on underachievement and the grade-point average criterion are considered on page 18.

Teacher Effectiveness

An area in which the concepts of humanistic psychology, especially those concerning the development of the self-actualizing individual, might seem particularly relevant is that involving teaching effectiveness. Dandes (1966) empirically investigated the relationship between those constructs of psychological health measured by the POI and those value measures—such as the *Minnesota Teacher Attitude Inventory* (Cook, Leeds, & Callis, 1953)—previously demonstrated to be related to teaching effectiveness. Positive correlations were obtained between POI scales and teachers' permissiveness and liberalism of educational viewpoints, as predicted. Correlations between the POI scales and measures of teacher attitude were all positive, ranging from .15 to .40. Negative correlations were obtained between POI scales and measures of authoritarianism and dogmatism. When the sample was dichotomized at the mean for POI Support and Time ratios, differences on all teacher attitude and value instruments were highly significant. Dandes concluded that the results clearly indicated a significant relationship between measured self-actualizing and important teacher attitudes and values: As predicted, the greater the actualizing, the greater the possession of attitudes and values characteristic of effective teaching.

In another study, Flanders (1969) reports significant correlations between the POI and teacher attitude in a sample of 129 elementary and secondary teachers. Correlations were all positive, ranging in magnitude from .12 to .47 (the latter being against the Time Competence scale). In that study teachers were involved in a sensitivity training program conducted during the course of a year. The POI was administered at the beginning and end of the program and as a follow-up. Significant change in the direction of self-actualizing was observed between the first and third administrations for eight of the twelve POI scales. The findings of McClain (1970a) further support the effect of mental health courses, focused especially on personal growth for the student, on the level of self-actualizing of teachers. Based on a sample of 130 teacher trainees, preto post-course changes reached significance for all twelve POI scales. Encounter group techniques, considered earlier in this volume, have also been applied effectively in educational settings. Using the POI as a pre- and post-treatment measure among a group of high-school educators involved in human relations training, Banmen and Capelle (1972) obtained significant increases on the major Inner-Directed (I) scale and five of the subscales following a three-day human relations training program. Furthermore, these changes were maintained over time, with scores obtained three months following the training showing the same scales to be significantly higher and, in addition, the Spontaneity subscale reaching significance.

In contrasting teachers who aspire to be administrators with career teachers, Mace (1970) found the former to be more self-actualizing as reflected by higher Inner-Directed scale scores. Similarly, among a sample of freshmen enrolled in an introductory teacher-education course, Pines (1970) found that, under instructor-centered conditions, the more self-actualizing students tended to have a less-favorable attitude toward a career in teaching and, further, that the more self-actualizing students displayed a greater mastery of the subject.

In a study relating aspects of the psychological health of elementary-school principals to the organizational climate of the school, Ford (1966) concluded that principals serving open-climate schools exhibited a higher level of self-actualizing than principals serving closed-climate schools. The open-climate principals demonstrated a greater acceptance of their own aggressiveness, greater self-acceptance, and greater capacity for intimate contact than the principals serving closed-climate schools.

Normative data for various educationally related samples are presented in Figure 12.

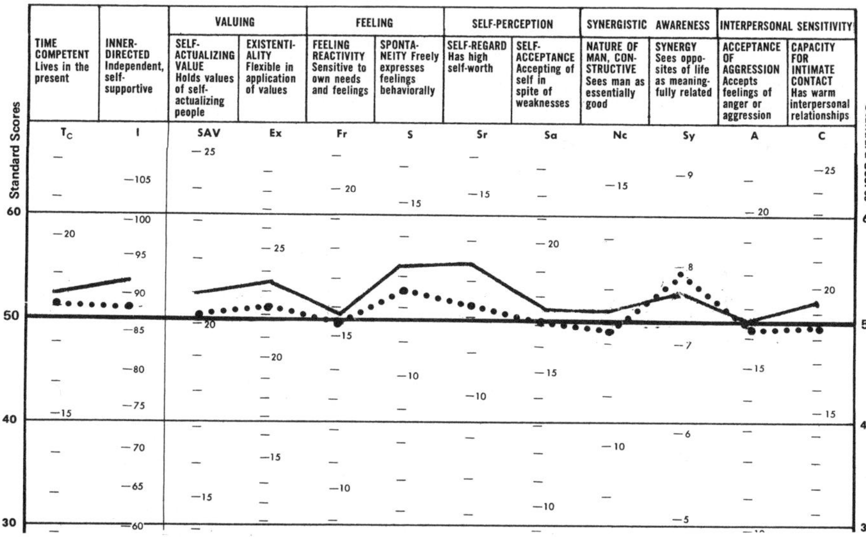

	Tc	I	SAV	Ex	Fr	S	Sr	Sa	Nc	Sy	A	C
Educational Consultants (—) (N=16)												
m	18.4	91.6	21.0	23.2	15.8	13.2	13.4	17.7	12.6	7.6	16.4	19.1
σ	2.1	14.2	3.7	4.4	3.5	3.8	2.2	4.3	1.3	1.2	3.8	4.0
Teachers (- - -) (N=120)												
m	18.0	87.3	20.2	22.2	15.7	12.7	12.2	17.0	12.3	7.9	16.1	18.5
σ	2.8	12.1	2.8	4.8	3.0	2.7	2.3	3.7	1.8	6.7	3.8	3.9

Based on data reported by Lafferty (1969)

Figure 12. POI Profiles for Educational Consultant and Teacher Samples.

An important question concerns what effect the level of self-actualizing of the teacher may have on the learning process. Problems of experimental design and appropriate controls have made the study of this more sensitive issue difficult. While Coble and Hounshell (1972) found no relationship between teacher level of self-actualizing and student achievement in biology, Coble (1973), in a more recent study involving 424 biology students and eighteen teachers, found significant differences in self-actualizing between those teachers whose students showed significant gains in critical thinking as contrasted with those whose students evidenced nonsignificant changes in critical thinking.

The POI has been used in the evaluation of a number of teaching and training techniques. Among those described previously have been the use of a videotape-feedback training model for teaching interpersonal relations skills by paraprofessionals (Archer & Kagan, 1973) and the number of studies evaluating encounter group techniques summarized in Table 2.

An interesting application of the POI is reported by Potkay (1973), in which simulated test-taking was employed as a teaching technique. Using this technique, undergraduate psychology students took the POI under standard instructions and then, following completion of assigned readings about a target person, again completed the POI under simulated conditions in which they were instructed to adopt the mental set of the target person. Results were reported on instructions to simulate Freud, Hemingway, and Jenny. Differences of POI profiles based on the three simulated conditions were clearly discernible, with Hemingway comparatively perceived as most self-actualizing and Jenny least actualizing. POI profiles based on the three simulated conditions are presented in Figure 13. Results of the study were held as supporting the usefulness of simulated test-taking in systematizing, objectifying, and differentiating student perceptions of the target person. Potkay suggests that the technique allows students to incorporate their own personal conclusions and background into their "understanding" of the person and that feedback in the form of individual and class profiles allows students to compare their inventory profiles with those of the person under study as well as with their peers.

Industry

The concepts of humanistic psychology have recently been brought to bear, at a theoretical level, on business organizational theory. Maslow's (1965) journal of impressions based on his 1962 observations of a California electronics plant resulted in a theoretical framework on which research in the area of self-actualizing as applied to industrial organizations could proceed. The development, during the same period, of the POI as an objective measure of self-actualizing, made possible the testing of specific hypotheses based on the theory.

One of the earliest applications of the POI in an industrial setting was that by Margulies (1969). This study was concerned with effects of organizational climate on employee self-actualizing and was undertaken at the same time (and location) that Abraham Maslow was gathering material for his book *Eupsychian Management* (1965). The major theoretical assump-

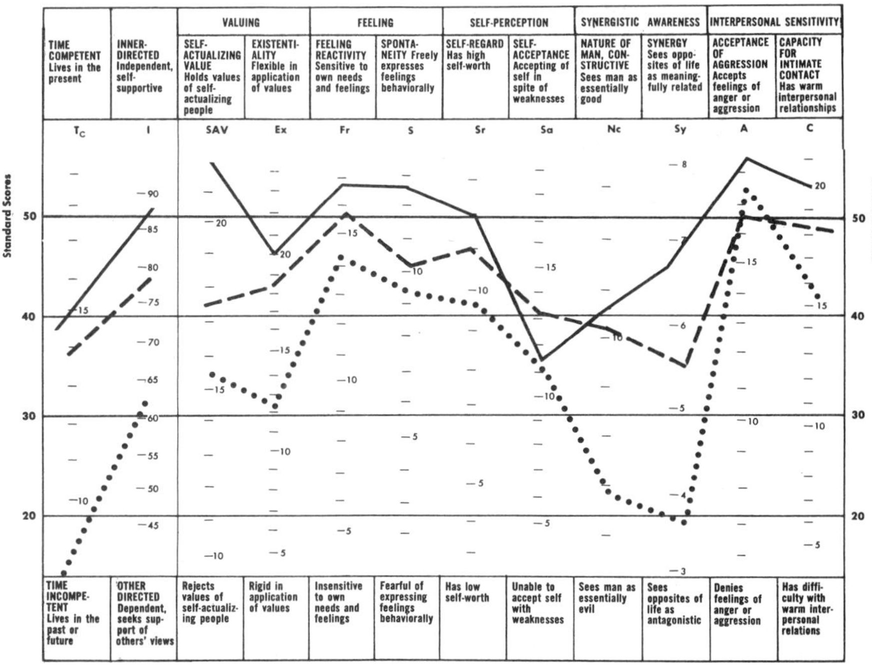

Figure 13. POI Profiles Based on Simulated Test-Taking Conditions for Freud, Hemmingway, and Jenny.

tion examined in the Margulies study was that a specific organizational culture—defined in terms of a specific set of values, attitudes, and behavioral norms—can contribute to the degree to which individuals become actualizing.

Results were interpreted as providing evidence of the possibility of identifying and describing organizational cultures that are associated with particular degrees of individual psychological growth. Data supported the hypotheses by defining two different sociotechnical systems, differentiating them in terms of existing organizational cultures, and identifying the specific cultural elements that correlate with increased psychological growth.

Several specific conclusions included (1) that a positive relationship exists between value-orientations and self-actualizing—the more intrinsic the value-orientation, the more psychological growth; (2) that higher self-actualizing groups do exhibit more awareness of the interconnectedness between task achievement and social-need satisfaction; and (3) that the behavior of the more self-actualizing groups is less determined by formal structure, formal role prescriptions, or formal authority.

A number of studies in industrial settings have concerned themselves with the relationship of self-actualizing to various occupational groups and to levels of functioning within an organization. Ladenberger (1971) administered the POI to 225 individuals selected from top and middle levels of management and representing different industries and all sections of the country. While performances at these two contiguous management levels were quite similar on the POI, statistically significant differences were obtained on the Self-Actualizing Value and Self-Regard subscales, with top-level managers scoring higher on the POI than middle-level managers. Profiles for these samples are presented in Figure 14. Normative data from other occupational samples have been reported by Lafferty (1969). Data for some of these samples are presented in Figures 14 and 15, while others are presented in Figure 12 in the section on Education and Figure 32 in the section on Reliability.

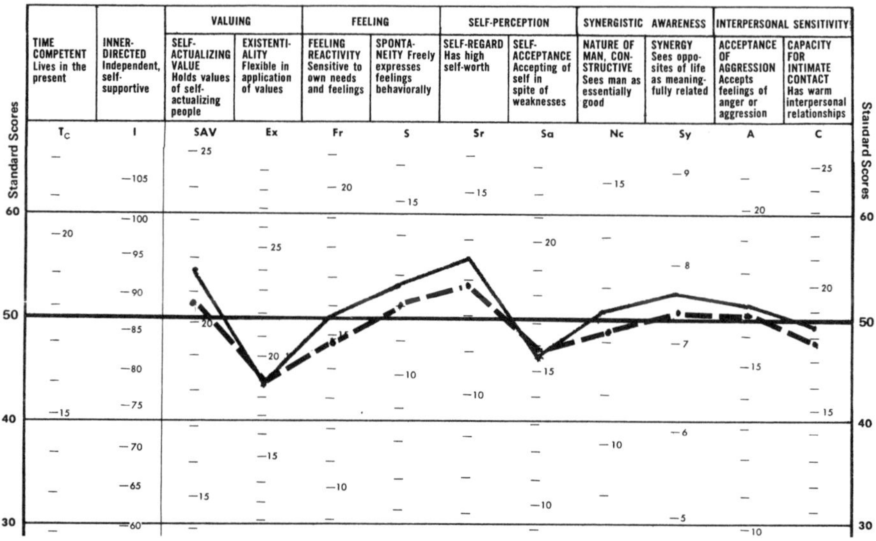

	SAV	Ex	Fr	S	Sr	Sa	Nc	Sy	A	C
Top Management (—) (N=116)										
m	21.6	18.8	15.3	12.6	13.5	15.6	12.5	7.6	17.0	18.1
σ	2.3	4.4	2.2	2.4	1.7	3.3	1.6	1.2	2.8	2.8
Middle Management (- - -) (N=108)										
m	20.5	18.8	14.9	12.0	12.9	15.8	12.1	7.4	16.6	17.9
σ	2.7	3.9	2.4	2.1	1.9	3.5	1.4	1.1	2.9	3.2

From Ladenberger (1971). Means for T_C and I not reported.

Figure 14. POI Profiles for Top and Middle Management Personnel.

Lessner and Knapp (1974) have reported data concerned with application of the POI in testing hypotheses concerning levels of self-actualizing of small-business owners. Previous observations among small-business entrepreneurs (Smith, 1967) led to the hypothesis that there are at least two types of entrepreneurs, which can be differentiated on the basis of orientation and characteristic behavior patterns. These Smith defined as craftsman-entrepreneur and opportunistic-entrepreneur. The craftsman-entrepreneur is described as perceiving and reacting to a limited range of culture and is characterized by narrowness of education, low social awareness, lack of flexibility in dealing with economic and social environments, and time orientation limited to present and past. The opportunistic-entrepreneur on

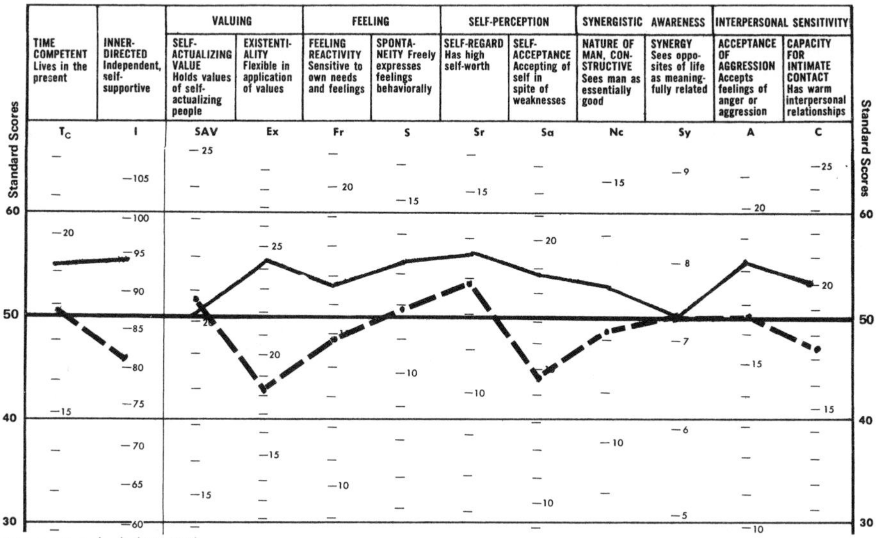

	Tc	I	SAV	Ex	Fr	S	Sr	Sa	Nc	Sy	A	C
Executive (—) (N=13)												
m	19.2	94.1	20.2	24.2	16.7	13.3	13.6	18.9	13.0	7.2	18.1	20.0
σ	2.0	10.3	2.5	3.1	2.9	1.8	2.3	2.8	1.4	1.0	2.9	3.1
Upper Middle Management (- - -) (N=59)												
m	17.4	81.1	21.2	18.1	14.9	11.9	12.9	14.6	12.1	7.2	16.3	17.2
σ	2.7	10.3	2.5	4.0	2.6	2.5	1.8	3.2	1.7	1.3	2.7	3.4

Based on data reported by Lafferty (1969)

Figure 15. POI Profiles for Executive and Upper Middle Management Samples.

the other hand is described as perceiving and reacting to a broad range of culture and is characterized by breadth of education, high social awareness and involvement, high flexibility in dealing with environments, and time orientation in the future. These concepts closely parallel certain of those held to represent self-actualizing behavior as measured by the POI.

The Lessner and Knapp (1974) study tested the hypothesis that merchandising-oriented (opportunistic) entrepreneurs would appear to be more self-actualizing than craft-oriented entrepreneurs. A sample of forty-two small-business owners were identified through a demographic questionnaire and interviews as either craft-oriented or merchandizing-oriented entrepreneurs. The POI Inner-Directed scale was significantly higher (.01 confidence level) for the merchandizing-entrepreneur group than the craftsman-entrepreneur group, thus supporting the hypothesis. The Spontaneity subscale also differentiated the groups at the .01 confidence level. Four other subscales, Self-Actualizing Values, Existentiality, Feeling Reactivity, and Capacity for Intimate Contact, significantly differentiated the groups at the .05 level. Thus, merchandizing-oriented entrepreneurs are seen to be more self-actualizing than craftsmen-oriented entrepreneurs. Profiles for these samples are presented in Figure 16.

As Maslow (1971) stated about the nomological network of data generated from the POI, and building up from his theory of self-

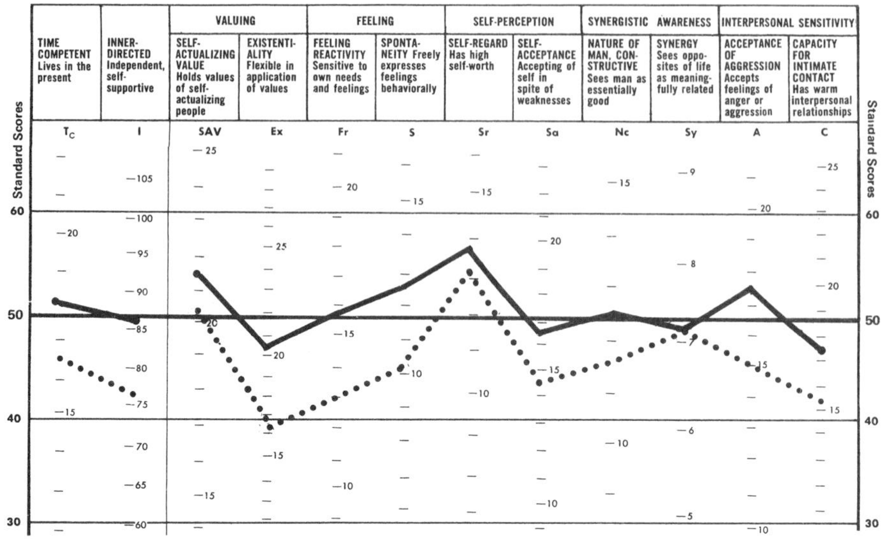

	Tc	I	SAV	Ex	Fr	S	Sr	Sa	Nc	Sy	A	C
Merchant Entrepreneur (—) (N=20)												
m	18.0	86.8	21.4	20.6	15.8	12.6	13.9	16.2	12.4	7.2	17.6	17.4
σ	2.4	7.9	2.2	4.2	2.8	2.2	1.6	3.1	1.6	.8	3.0	2.9
Craftsman Entrepreneur (- - -) (N=20)												
m	16.6	75.6	20.2	16.6	13.0	10.2	13.3	14.3	11.7	7.2	15.0	15.3
σ	2.5	7.3	2.5	3.6	2.5	2.0	1.4	3.9	1.3	1.3	2.5	2.2

From Lessner and Knapp (1974)

Figure 16. POI Profiles for Merchant Oriented and Craftsman Oriented Entrepreneur Samples.

actualization, "It correlates well with external variables of various kinds and keeps on accumulating additional correlational meanings" (p. 28). Data from Lessner and Knapp (1974) add further support to hypotheses arising from the theory. In the above-described application of the POI to samples from the business world, data suggest that small-business entrepreneurs are not an entirely homogeneous population. Samples identified through demographic characteristics, and hypothesized to differ on variables of self-actualizing, can be distinguished by POI scales. There appears to be a relationship among personal characteristics of the entrepreneur, the type of firm built, and the growth of this firm. Thus, measurement and statistical techniques are seen to support previous case-study observations of small-business entrepreneurs (such as those of Smith, 1967).

Maslow (1965) has suggested that eupsychian, enlightened management policies based on humanistic theories are necessary for interacting with a growing, actualizing population. Present data suggest such a relationship among small businesses. As businesses grow, these concepts may be expected to play an even larger role in formulation of management policies. The expanded use of the POI in measuring effects of organizational-sponsored encounter groups would seem to reflect a growing awareness on the part of organizations of the desirability of fostering personal growth.

Maslow (1965, p. 263), in considering Drucker's (1954) organizational structure, has suggested the Ninth Vice President, reflecting the eventual desirability of coordinating the principles of eupsychian management under one manager responsible for wide philosophical, psychological, and psychotherapeutic and educational training.

Prediction of adaptation to a foreign culture is a problem of concern to many business, as well as religious, governmental, and educational, institutions with international affiliations. Uhes and Shybut (1971) investigated the relationship between POI scores and success in Peace Corps training programs in Micronesia. Using a sample of ninety-two, significant relationship were found for the two major scales and four of the POI subscales against Peace Corps Final Selection Board rating following a ten-week training program. Correlations ranged in magnitude up to .41 against the Inner-Directed scale.

Application of the concepts of actualizing measured by the POI in business and industrial settings provide some of the most exciting and varied areas for study. As Ladenberger (1971) notes in her summary of literature in this area, "Work and business are central to American life" (p. 23). Few other countries are as work-oriented as the United States. As Menninger (in Neff, 1968) has stated, "Three-fourths of the patients who come to psychiatrists are suffering from an incapacity of their satisfaction in work or their inability to work. For many it is their chief complaint" (p. 94). Indeed, the very psychological identity of a man or woman is inextricably woven in and through the personal meaning of his or her work.

By its very nature, self-actualizing, as applied to entrepreneurial orientations, involves what is popularly know as "doing your own thing." This was graphically demonstrated by Lessner and Knapp (1974) when they distinguished between the craftsman entrepreneur and the opportunist extrepreneur. The Inner-Directed scale of the POI was able to differentiate between these two entrepreneurial orientations by describing the craftsman as a combination of a tradition-oriented and an inner-directed person. The opportunist, by contrast, was shown to be a similar combination of other-directedness and inner-directedness. Clearly, in both cases, the entrepreneurial function relates to the inner-directed, self-guided aspect of the entrepreneur's personality. The craftsman, tradition-guided to take pride in the quality of his or her individual production, and the other-directed opportunist, adjusting to the realities of the economic marketplace (itself a reflection of the demands and values of others), were pointed up by the I scale of the POI and by other subscales. The tradition orientation relates more to the product and the other orientation to the needs of the consuming public, with its broader implications and individual variations.

The face of industry is turning from the vicarious motivations of survival and power-seeking to the search for greater wealth of personal satisfaction and fulfillment, enjoyed by manager and employee alike, in the creation of a society within the industrial setting that can afford the opportunity for emotional growth as well as the more practical means of personal sustenance.

Religion

Maslow (1971), in commenting on an earlier book, *Religious Values and Peak-Experiences* (1964), suggests that the work was "too imbalanced toward the individualistic and too hard on groups, organizations and communites." He then proceeds to develop the notion that the need for community belongingness is itself a basic need that can be fulfilled only through contact with other human beings (i.e., society) and poses the questions, "How good a society does human nature permit?" and, "How good a human nature does society permit?" A recent large-scale examination of the American Catholic Priesthood (Greely, 1970) contains some evidence of the degree of supportiveness of a major societal institution to self-actualizing. Among the major findings of this study were significant correlations between the POI Inner-Directed scale (the primary overall measure of self-actualizing) and the following variables that reflect on the supportiveness of the Church on certain values:

	Correlation
Conflict between real and ideal distribution of power in Church	.19
Need to reform Church exercise of initiative	.38
Unfavorable reaction to birth control encyclical	.35
Traditional values scale	-.43
Plan to stay in priesthood	-.28

Thus, among American priests, higher levels of actualizing are seen to be associated with perceived conflict among present and ideal distribution of power, felt need to reform the Church with respect to the exercise of personal initiative, and an unfavorable reaction to the birth control encyclical. Further, those relatively more self-actualizing priests tend not to hold to more traditional values and are less apt to plan to stay in the priesthood. Supporting this latter correlation are data comparing POI scores of a sample of 917 active priests. Scores were higher among the resigned priests on every POI measure of self-actualizing. Data in this study tend to suggest that changes within the Church are necessary if the goal is to maximize institutional support of the self-actualizing process.

In fact, in the study above, those who resigned from the priesthood were significantly higher on all POI scales than those staying in, again perhaps reflecting the incompatibility of Church structure and the self-actualizing of its members. Profiles for these samples are presented in Figure 17.

Other studies have emanated from the American Catholic Priesthood study described by Kennedy and Heckler (1971). Among these studies is that by Murphy (1972), in which a stratified sample of 218 priests selected from the larger sample was used to examine the relationship of POI scores to a measure of adjustment covering areas such as self-perception, interpersonal relations, and satisfaction gained through religion, priesthood, and job.

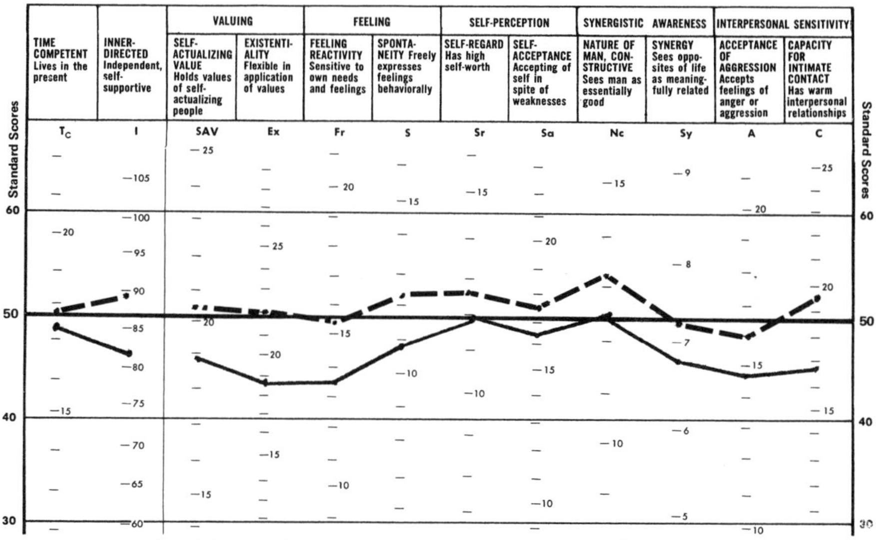

Active Priests (- - -) (N=917)

m 17.2 81.0 18.9 18.8 13.5 10.8 11.8 16.3 12.3 6.8 14.9 16.9

Resigned Priests (—) (N=270)

m 17.8 89.4 20.3 22.0 15.4 12.3 12.7 17.3 13.1 7.3 16.0 19.4

Based on data reported by Greely (1970)

Figure 17. POI Profiles for Active Priests and Resigned Priests.

Although not identical in content, the magnitude of correlations was highest between POI scales and adjustment measures of self-perception, interpersonal relations, and psychological maturity. All POI scales were significantly related to the latter two variables. In evaluating adjustment in terms of satisfaction with Church, priesthood, and job, the POI major scale of Time Competence and subscale Self-Regard were significantly, and negatively, related to all three criteria. Thus, greater Time Competence and higher Self-Regard are seen to be associated with dissatisfaction with Church, role, and job.

Webster and Stewart (1969) report results from administration of the POI to a sample of seventy-seven ministers in the Baptist Union of New Zealand. Ministers' scores were compared with POI scores from a group of 853 young adults in New Zealand. Although differences were not large in most instances, they were found to be significantly higher for the ministers on the Time Competence, Self-Acceptance, Spontaneity, and Capacity for Intimate Contact scales, and lower on the Synergy scale. Scores for theological liberalism and conservatism were also obtained for the ministers and related to POI scores. Ministers scoring higher on theological conservatism were comparatively non-self-actualizing, especially dependent [negative correlations with Inner-Direction (I) scale; rigid, Existentiality (Ex); insensitive, Feeling Reactivity (Fr); rejecting of the constructiveness of human nature, Nature of Man (Nc); and poorer in interpersonal relationships, Capacity for Intimate Contact (C)]. Scores for a dogmatism scale were also related to the

POI. Ministers scoring low in dogmatism were significantly more self-actualizing on all scales except Self-Regard (Sr). The authors found support for the expectation that ministers who were theologically liberal, open-minded and more psychologically healthy would express more role conflict. The authors conclude that the religiously conservative minister typically falls far short of the "abundant life" and that the results of their study suggest benefits to be derived from a new emphasis on psychological health of ministers.

Two studies discussed previously have reported on the use of the POI with ministers involved in sensitivity training programs. Byrd (1966; 1967) used the POI in a pre- and post-treatment design with 131 professional church workers to evaluate the comparative effectiveness of sensitivity training procedures and other procedures collectively designated as "creative risk taking." Using an analysis of variance design, significant differences between experimental treatment groups were obtained for the major POI Inner-Directed (I) and four subscales.

Reddy (1972b) obtained data to support the hypothesis that human relations sensitivity training groups among missionary samples can be composed of preselected individuals whose interpersonal compatibility styles affect the outcome of their personal growth. Among the forty interdenominational missionaries participating in a five day sensitivity training program, trainees in two incompatible affection groups gained significantly more on the major Inner-Directed (I), scale and subscales of Feeling Reactivity (Fr), Spontaneity (S) and Capacity for Intimate Contact (C) than trainees in two compatible affection groups.

In any profession or life endeavor with which an actualizing person might seek to identify himself, there is an inevitable movement from the early, more stable and rigid sense of tradition orientation described by Riesman et al. (1950) to a greater self-directedness. This movement must continue into the further area of other-directedness in which individuals, to define their existential essence within the context of the society or organization in which they dwell, see their greatest opportunity for growth in a sort of dynamic equilibrium, centered on inner-directedness but also involving, as the situation demands, other orientations. This is analogous to living in the present while utilizing the past as a kind of datum for extrapolation in moving through each new moment and simultaneously being cognizant of the future as the time where self-actualizing dreams and goals reside. Both of these self-actualizing concepts are measured by the Inner-Directed and the Time Competence scales of the POI.

Constraints imposed by the organization on this essential dynamism are reflected by opposition to established rules and an opting of freedom from the rigidity of church dogmas and regulations to a greater flexibility and realism. Greely's (1970) study exemplifies this condition in the area of religion, and the POI ably demonstrated its ability to identify the actualizing priest, in constrast to those more hidebound by tradition who, by clinging to the established precepts of the ecclesiastical past, seek a fictitious security in the present. The social demands on religions are changing, and with them, greater opportunities for actualizing are being demanded. Increasingly, more and more freedom to grow is being granted to pastor and priest by those who control the form of the religious disciplines and who are coming to recognize the inevitability of this movement. The POI, as the above studies have clearly shown, separates the dynamic from the conservative and describes in quantitative terms the characteristics of the growth-oriented and innovative self-actualizers among the servants of the church.

Beyond the recognition of concepts of actualizing important to those working within the organizational structure of the church are the tremendous opportunities for the introduction and teaching of such concepts to congregations. Again, applications of group techniques within this context, as exemplified by the research of Byrd (1967), illustrate the educational potential within the church.

Other Societal Institutions

Beyond the implications of POI research for institutions of school, business, and church presented above, are results from samples that are perhaps best characterized as challenging the established mores of contemporary society. These results, based on studies of young-adult samples, provide an interesting insight into the dynamics of concepts of self-actualizing. Freeman and Brubaker (1971) compared POI results from participants in a campus demonstration with those of nonparticipants. POI responses from fifty-four college demonstrators who staged a sit-in to protest the administration's questioning of a liberalized alcohol-on-campus policy were compared with the responses of fifty-four student non-demonstrators. Significant differences were obtained between the samples on the two major scales and nine of the ten subscales, with non-demonstrators scoring significantly higher only on the Nature of Man-Constructive scale and the demonstrators scoring higher on the remaining POI scales. Profiles are presented in Figure 18. Based on the POI results, Freeman and Brubaker concluded that those students who are "unwilling to quietly accept what they perceive to be injustices in the world around them bear a closer resemblance to the type of student our colleges and universities seek to develop" (p. 464).

In a study of the mental health of persons selecting a "deviant" family form, Constantine and Constantine (1973) administered the POI to an unselected sample of forty participants in multilateral marriages. As the authors note, departure from the norms in marriage and family structure are frequently perceived as threatening to the fabric of society. In the multilateral marriage, three or more conjugal partners perceive themselves as being married to—or having an analogous commitment to—at least two other partners. There are no strictly monogamous relationships in the group. Perhaps due to the extreme divergence of this emerging family form the question has been raised among professionals as to the emotional health of participants in the multilateral marriage. Data from the above described sample were used to construct a POI profile in which the median scores, as

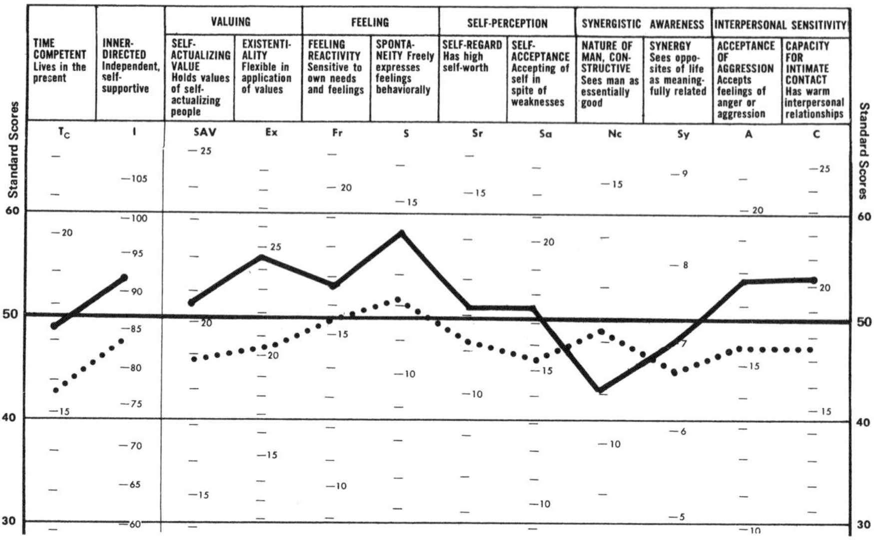

Demonstrators (—) (N=54)

m	17.2	91.5	20.6	24.8	16.9	14.0	12.2	17.5	11.0	7.0	17.8	20.2
σ	3.0	9.7	2.6	4.2	2.4	2.4	2.2	3.9	2.7	1.3	1.8	3.4

Non-Demonstrators (- - -) (N=158)

m	15.6	84.0	18.9	20.1	15.6	12.0	11.4	15.3	12.3	6.6	15.8	17.6
σ	2.7	12.8	3.1	4.6	3.3	3.3	2.3	4.0	2.2	1.4	3.2	4.2

From Freeman and Brubaker (1971)

Figure 18. POI Profiles Based on Samples of Campus Demonstrators and Non-Demonstrators.

well as the range of the middle 50 percent of scores, are compared with the "normal" adult POI norms. This profile is presented in Figure 19. Conclusions drawn from the comparisons made in this study were that participants in multilateral marriage were not representative of a pathologic population and that the conjecture that the marital/sexual "deviance" reflected in multilateral marriages implies pathlogy should be rejected.

To examine the assumption that children are essential for the happiness and fulfillment of married couples, Hersch (1973) compared the POI scores of a parent sample consisting of thirty-three married couples who had children with a nonparent sample consisting of thirty-two married couples who had decided not to have children. The Inner-Directed scale was significantly higher for the nonparent sample and the mean POI profile for that sample was above the parent sample on all scales except Nature of Man, as shown in Figure 20. Regarding the reversal on the Nature of Man scale it is interesting to speculate on the dynamics of this underlying characteristic found among the nonparent sample as well as among the demonstrator sample reported in Figure 18. Although the study suffered from sampling difficulties for these populations, Hersch suggests that the results might seem to cast doubt on the cultural assumption that adults must have children to be self-actualizing.

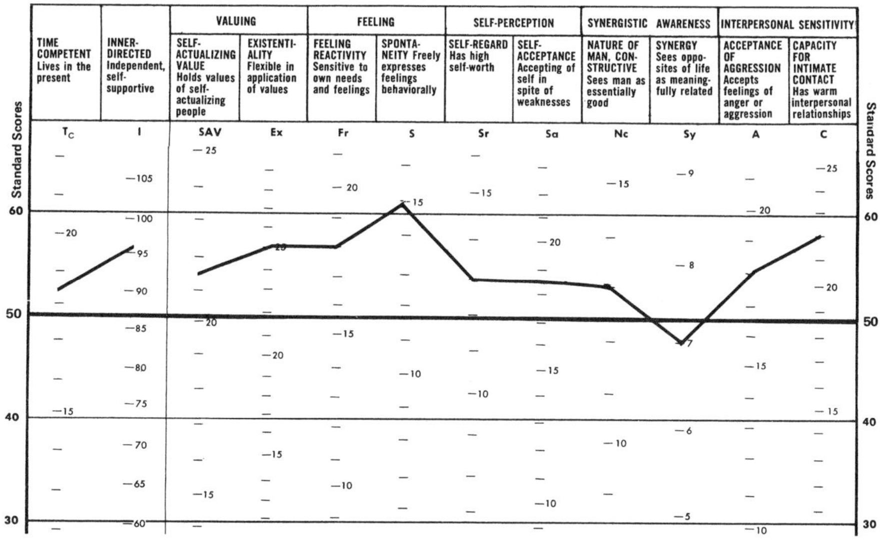

Figure 19. POI Profile for Participants in Multilateral Marriages based on median scores reported by Constantine and Constantine (1973).

The relationship of self-actualizing to attitudes toward women's rights and roles in society was examined by Hjelle and Butterfield (1974). Mean POI scores were compared for two groups of college females in an introductory psychology course, one a sample of twenty with liberal attitudes toward women's role in society, and the other a sample of twenty with conservative attitudes. Ten of the twelve POI scales were significantly higher for those with liberal, profeminist attitudes as contrasted with those expressing more tradition-bound attitudes.

In a related study by Doyle (1975), POI scores were correlated with a feminist-antifeminist attitude scale. The hypothesis was that self-actualizing males and females would be more apt to express attitudes of a profeminist, nontraditional, and egalitarian nature toward women and their social roles. This hypothesis was based on Maslow's (1970) contention that relationships with women for self-actualizing males would be different from those of non-self-actualizing males in that the actualizing males would "be more easy and free and familiar and impolite in the traditional sense" (p. 196). Results indicated that profeminist attitudes were positively and significantly related to actualizing. Based on a total sample of 150, significant correlations against all POI scales were positive. Correlations ranged in magnitude up to .45 between profeminist attitudes and the POI subscale Capacity for Intimate Contact. Other relationships of similar magnitude were obtained against POI scales of Existentiality, Inner-Directed, and Feeling Reactivity.

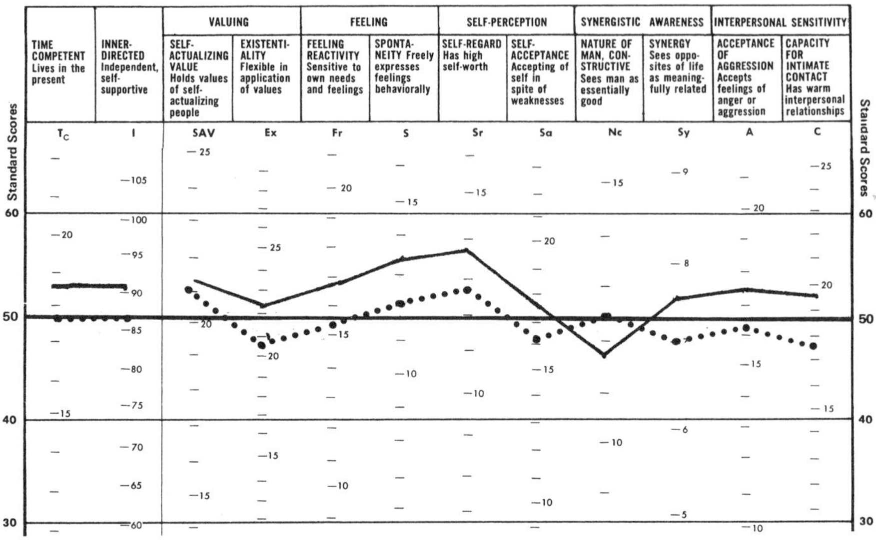

	Tc	I	SAV	Ex	Fr	S	Sr	Sa	Nc	Sy	A	C
Non-Parents (—) (N=64)												
m	18.5	90.5	21.2	22.3	16.8	13.2	13.7	17.5	11.8	7.4	17.3	19.4
σ	2.7	11.3	2.4	4.6	3.0	2.7	1.6	3.5	1.8	1.2	3.2	3.8
Parents (- - -) (N=66)												
m	17.6	85.2	21.1	20.3	15.1	12.0	12.8	16.1	12.3	7.0	16.1	17.4
σ	3.2	11.2	2.7	4.1	3.1	2.7	2.0	3.4	1.7	1.1	3.3	3.5

From Hersch (1973)

Figure 20. POI Profiles for a Sample of Married Couples Deciding Not to Have Children and a Sample of Parent Couples.

The results of these studies, considered in conjunction with others concerning the relationship of institutional practices to levels of actualizing, such as the American Catholic Priesthood study presented earlier (p. 48), illustrate the relationship of more liberal attitudes and social activism to higher levels of actualizing as measured by the POI.

Nowhere is the movement away from rigid tradition orientation perceived more clearly than in the applications of the POI to innovators and instigators of social change. The study of Freeman and Brubaker (1971) utilized the POI to compare the active, liberally minded campus demonstrators with those staid and conservative spectators who, by adhering to established college policies, disclosed their orientation to the past and to traditional values. Again, Hersch (1973) was able to distinguish marriage partners electing not to bring children into the world from the more conventionally minded couples who were anticipating their future lives within the context of home and children. Here, again, the POI was able to show a trend toward the inner- versus other-directedness—the former being the more self-actualizing. The entire POI profiles were upwardly mobile in the cases of these respondents. The active decision of these, perhaps more aware, couples may reflect a movement away from the traditional hearth-and-home concept of the past.

The tendency, among female college students, to actualize was confirmed by Hjelle and Butterfield (1974) for those female college students espousing the newer, more liberal concepts of equal rights for women, and a nonsexist society, to which the more traditional citizenry are at least passively opposed. Social change, when evolving in the direction of greater freedom of opportunity to self-actualize and to develop individual potentialities, can be detected and quantified by the POI. It is interesting to conjecture what the POI would have indicated could it have been used to compare present-day politicians and statesmen with their counterparts of two hundred years ago. Perhaps the latter would have achieved higher scores on the major POI scales and at least on the majority of subscales, thus indicating the courage and flexibility of the framers of the Constitution to flaunt authority and tradition and to champion the freedom and the rights of the individual citizen.

Medicine

Prediction of criteria of success in nurses' training is a use to which the POI has been put in a number of studies. Green (1967) related POI scores from a sample of sophomore student nurses to several criteria, including grade-point average, clinical-practice grade, and satisfaction with nursing. It was concluded that in addition to scholastic aptitude certain aspects of actualizing contributed to success in nursing, among those being time orientation in the present (Time Competence), expression of feelings (Spontaneity), the perceived ability to transcend dichotomies in understanding others and self (Synergy), and a high regard for self because of recognized strengths (Self-Regard). In clinical situations, POI variables of Synergy and Spontaneity were more highly related to the criteria than scholastic aptitude.

Ilardi and May (1968) found that among a group of student nurses responding to the POI over a three-year period, significant growth in the direction of self-actualizing occurs especially during the first year. The changes were in the direction of greater acceptance of self and others, greater awareness and acceptance of feelings, and a more flexible application of values. Results of administration upon entrance into the nursing program and at the end of the third year are presented in Figure 21. Significant relationships were also found between family income and increases in POI scores—low income being associated with larger increases and high income with smaller increases. Shimmin (1969) found the public-health staff nurses in the category of twenty-five years of age or less were in the self-actualizing range on the POI profile while the group of twenty-six- to thirty-five-year-old nurses were below the mean norm self-actualizing score for every scale except Nature of Man.

In an extensive study of role adaptation among baccalaureate degree nurses, Kramer, McDonnell, and Reed (1972) found significant interaction effects among measures of actualizing from the POI and various indices of role conception and job success. The profile based on the total sample, as shown in Figure 21, follows very closely the normal adult sample. While

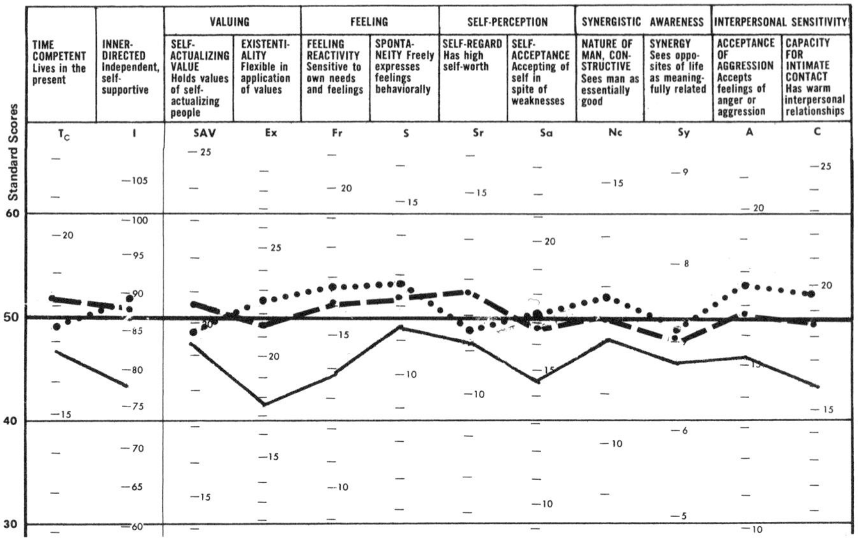

	T_C	I	SAV	Ex	Fr	S	Sr	Sa	Nc	Sy	A	C
Entering Nursing Students (N=41)												
m	16.8	77.3	19.2	17.5	13.9	11.2	11.1	14.6	12.0	6.8	15.1	16.0
SD	2.6	7.0	2.6	3.9	2.5	2.6	2.4	2.7	1.7	.9	2.8	2.7
End of Third Year Administration (N=41)												
m	17.3	89.2	19.8	22.4	16.8	12.7	11.5	17.1	12.9	7.2	17.4	19.8
SD	2.3	11.1	2.8	4.2	2.4	2.8	2.2	3.8	1.9	1.2	2.6	3.7

Based on data reported by Robert Ilardi (1975)

	T_C	I	SAV	Ex	Fr	S	Sr	Sa	Nc	Sy	A	C
Baccalaureate Degree Nurses (N=195)												
m	18.2	86.6	20.4	21.1	16.2	12.4	12.6	16.2	12.6	7.1	16.8	18.4

Based on data reported by Kramer, McDonnell and Reed (1972)
Standard deviations not reported.

Figure 21. POI Profiles for Student and Graduate Nurse Samples.

linear correlations between combinations of POI scales used in this study and indices of role perception were not significant, interaction effects did reach significance. The authors note that statements concerning the effects of role conception on self-actualizing should be made with reference to the rated level of success of the nurses.

In the professional vocation of nursing, as an adjunct to the field of applied medicine, several investigations, as noted above, were able to employ the POI to good advantage. Clearly, the initial decision to become a nurse can be based on a variety of motives ranging from a desire for job security, through altruistic reasons, to an inclination toward self-transcendency in the sense that Frankl (1959) speaks in his *Man's Search for Meaning*. It scarcely can be argued that to find a purpose in one's life implies emotional growth and therefore a will to self-actualize, even though it might, in the case of nursing, seem to imply other-directedness. A moment's consideration, however, will confirm that to serve others in a manner that is based on personal choice is in fact a sign of inner-directedness. Taken together with the higher scores on Time Competence, Spontaneity, Synergy, and Self-Regard, as in the Green (1967) study, this indicates a greater awareness of self and of one's contact boundary with the environment, and an ambition to develop potentially within the context of this chosen profession. The POI's indication of higher self-actualizing among nurses of lower socioeconomic origins would seem to suggest a stronger drive to transcend the traditional materialistic values of social position by performing a humanitarian service from which greater self-satisfaction might be derived.

Adolescence

High-school samples have been the focus of several investigations utilizing the POI. In general, adolescent and early-college-age subjects score considerably lower on the POI than unselected adult samples. (A POI profile based on a high-school-age sample is presented in Figure 11.) This finding is consistent with Maslow's developmental theory of self-actualizing in which he stated that self-actualization of the sort observed in older people was not possible among young developing persons in our society. In his early selection of a self-actualizing college student sample for individual study, Maslow (1970, p. 150) selected only the healthiest one percent of the student population as representative.

Examining the relationship between self-actualizing, creativity, and intelligence among high-school students, Damm (1970), as described earlier, found that students who had obtained high scores on measures of both intelligence and creativity were more self-actualizing than those who had obtained a high score only on intelligence or creativity or on neither. In therms of self-actualizing, a high level of performance on either an intelligence scale or a creativity scale alone is not significantly better than a high level of performance on both. The author interpreted the implications of these results as calling for a curriculum in which development of both intellectual and creative abilities is stressed rather than concentration on one to the exclusion of the other.

Gerber (1964), examining the relationship between self-actualizing and creativity among community-college students, also reported positive relationships, with those scoring higher on the POI also scoring higher on certain dimensions tapped by measures of creativity.

Weber (1970) has presented POI data for large samples of Catholic-high-school girls homogeneously grouped according to ability levels within the ninth, tenth, eleventh, and twelfth grades. The groups of lower-ability students were generally found to score lower on POI scales.

In a study of the effects of maternal employment, same-sex chum denial in preadolescence, and residential mobility on self-actualizing of adolescents, Dawson (1969) found only the residential mobility variable to be related to self-actualizing. Students who had lived in either four or five communites since starting first grade scored significantly higher on the POI than those who had lived in fewer or in more communities.

Data from these studies as well as those based on adolescent samples described in the sections on Education, Psychopathology, and Drug Abuse demonstrate the relevance of concepts measured by the POI to behavior among adolescents. Thus, although as Maslow noted young adults do not tend to reach such high levels of actualization as may be found among older persons, the POI does differentiate among individuals in this age group. If it is borne in mind that one intent of measurement provided by the POI is to measure actualiz*ing* as a state rather than actualiz*ed* as a trait, interpretative usefulness of results is greatly enhanced. Those among youth who obtain comparatively high POI scores may be compared to those dozen or two college students among three thousand whom Maslow (1970, p. 150) described as "growing well." Shostrom, Knapp, and Knapp (1976) speak of the age thirty-five as the "high noon" of life and the few studies available to date bearing on this topic tend to bear this out. This topic is considered in greater detail in the section on Age-Related Trends.

It is interesting to consider the possible causal relationship between age and self-actualizing as measured by the POI. Studies of intelligence, creativity, and itineracy, such as those cited above, seem to provide a further clue to the basis for Maslow's contention regarding age and self-actualizing. Human development, after all, occurs over time and is a learning process strongly influenced both by exposure to changing life conditions and, as Eysenck (1973) maintains, by certain prevailing genetic predispositions. It would therefore seem to follow logically that the need to face comparative uncertainty during one's adolescent years, and to adjust repeatedly to different residential environments and social situations (as in the case of the military family), must compel increased awareness, a broadening knowledge of the world and social milieus (sometimes defined as intelligence), and stimulate, or at least conserve, innate creativity in the growing individual. That the POI did detect this tendency among certain respondents again confirms its ability to identify different levels of self-actualizing even among adolescents whose life spans have not yet provided that greater richness of experience possessed by many of their more self-actualizing age superiors.

Psychopathology

Of particular interest to those concerned with the theoretical implications—for humanistic concepts—of data obtained from the POI, are those studies involving psychopathic population. A criticism sometimes made of the self-actualizing concept is that, following many of these precepts to their logical extreme, the truly self-actualizing individual would be the psychopathic individual, completely egocentric and freed from self-imposed restrictions of society. Thus, finding that psychopathic samples scored as relatively self-actualizing would have serious implications for the theory. However, data collected do not support this contingency. Profiles based upon delinquent and felon samples generally show a pattern characteristic of nonactualizing individuals.

Data collected by Knapp—and reported in the POI Manual (Shostrom, 1974)—from a sample of eighty-four delinquent males in a Navy brig showed this sample to be below the norm mean on all POI scales. The POI profile for this sample is presented in Figure 22. Differences between this delin-

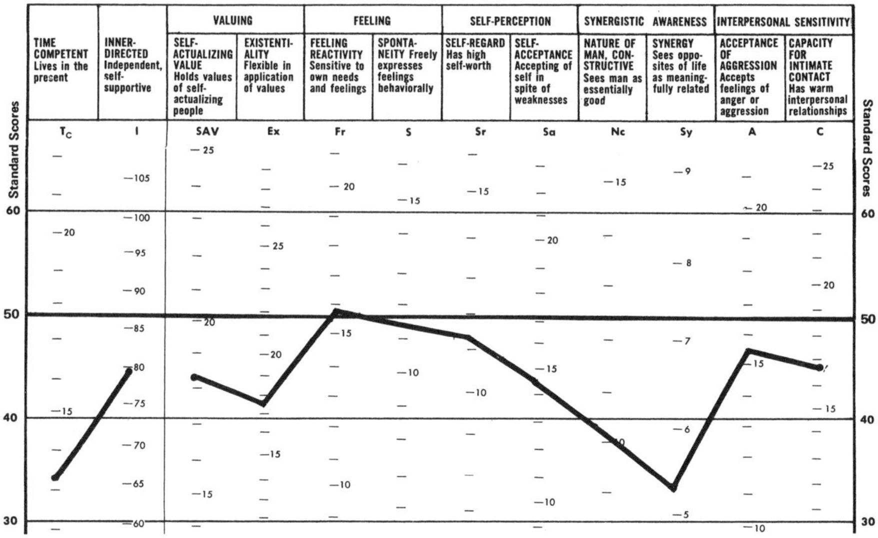

m	13.4	79.1	18.1	17.7	15.6	11.5	11.3	14.7	10.1	5.3	15.2	16.9
σ	2.6	9.6	2.8	5.2	3.0	2.3	2.1	3.5	2.0	1.6	3.3	3.5

Based on data reported by Robert R. Knapp (Shostrom, 1974)

Figure 22. POI Profile for a Navy Delinquent Sample Confined to a Navy Brig (N=84).

quent sample and the profile for the POI norm sample were greatest for the Time Competence scale and for the Synergy subscale, with the delinquents scoring about one and one-half standard deviations below the adult norm mean. The same pattern of differences appeared in comparing the Navy delinquents with a similar, but nondelinquent, Navy sample.

In a series of studies briefly described in the preceding section, Fisher (1968, 1973), Fisher and Silverstein (1969b), and Silverstein and Fisher (1974) have presented data obtained from incarcerated psychopathic felons relating to their levels of self-actualizing as well as to their attitudes toward society's view of values of self-actualizing individuals. The authors summarize these findings by suggesting that felons recognize the social acceptability of the self-actualizing concept but possess a distorted view of the norm, feeling that they are in fact more self-actualizing than is normal or socially acceptable in the culture. POI profiles based on an incarcerated-felon sample are presented in Figure 23.

When viewed together, profiles based on the several psychopathic samples available display markedly lower Time Competence scale scores as well as comparatively lower scores for Existentiality and for scales in the area of synergistic awareness.

Psychopathology is the investigation of mental disorders characterized by a deviance from culturally accepted norms and manifested by behaviors antithetical and detrimental to other members of society. In one sense, persons regarded as in some way psychopathic display certain personality traits that

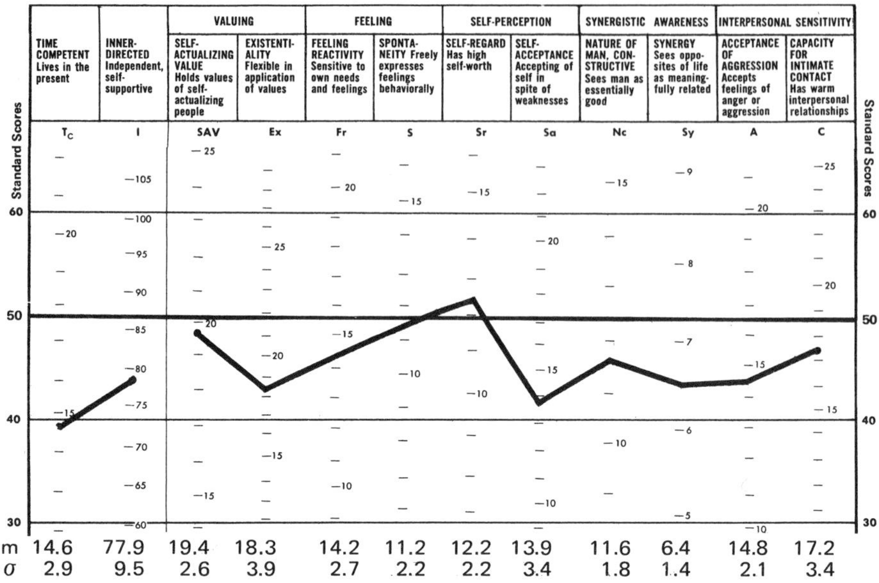

From Silverstein and Fisher (1973)

Figure 23. POI Profile for an Incarcerated Felon Sample (N=500).

suggest an inability to distinguish between external reality and internally generated fantasy. It is in regarding the latter as the more real that their behaviors seem to be based. That they are in some way freed from social restrictions is incorrect. That they are unable to clearly perceive these restrictions, and so act as though they were nonexistent, is more to the point. Perls (1973), in his *Gestalt Approach*, stated, "The paranoic has been found to be ... a highly aggressive personality who, unable to bear the responsibility for his own wishes, feelings and desires, attaches them to objects or people in the environment" (p. 35). This makes it possible to disavow the offensive personal aspects. By shifting the boundary between themselves and the rest of the world too much in their own favor, individuals become criminals. Perls again said that "the criminal is a man who has arrogated to himself functions traditionally defined as the prerogatives of the state. The man who arrogates these functions to himself is, in our society, a criminal" (p. 27).

Self-actualizing, while incorporating concepts of time presence and inner-directedness, also relates to tolerance, spontaneity, synergy, and other factors indicative of other-awareness and, indeed, of other-tolerance—factors that psychopaths consistently disregard. The POI illuminates these emotio-rational deficiencies in psychopaths and others who display deviant behavior. Thus, no inconsistency exists between what is inherent in the psychopathic condition and low scores, which, as the above studies affirm, have been obtained by many social deviants.

Alcoholism

Use of the POI with samples of alcoholics has provided some provocative findings for the theory of the actualizing person. While the POI has been used widely as a counseling device in alcoholic rehabilitation programs, results from only a few important applications have been submitted to statistical analysis. Weir (1965), Weir and Gade (1969), and Zaccaria and Weir (1967) reported a study involving seventy alcoholics and their spouses who were participating in an alcoholic treatment program. They found all mean POI scores for this sample to be significantly lower than the original validating, clinically nominated, self-actualizing sample. (The POI Profile based on this sample is presented in Figure 24.) Further, all but one scale showed the experimental treatment sample to be significantly lower than the normal adult sample reported by Shostrom. One scale, Time Competence, was significantly lower for the treatment group than for the nonactualizing sample. Apparently, the alcoholic in particular is apt to be the person dwelling on past or future events, lacking the full awareness, contact, and feeling reactivity of the more time competent person.

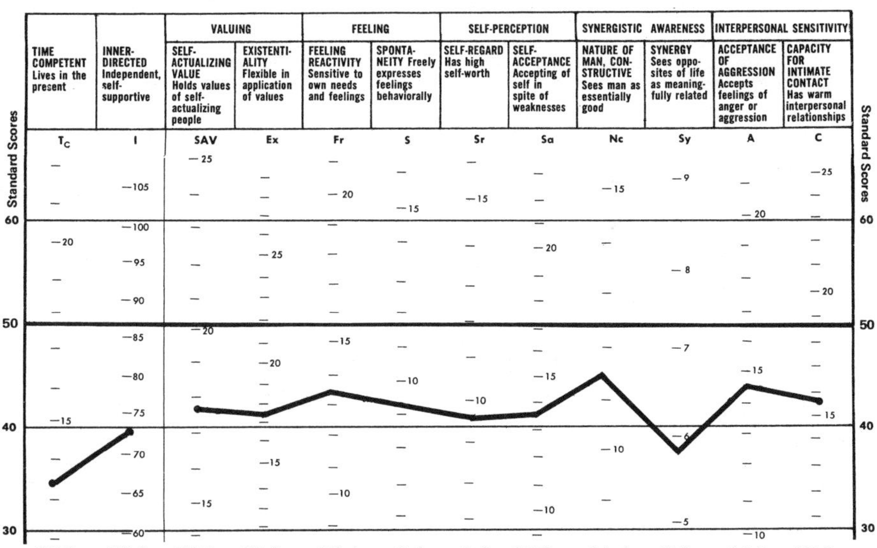

	T_c	I	SAV	Ex	Fr	S	Sr	Sa	Nc	Sy	A	C
m	13.3	72.9	17.7	17.2	13.4	9.1	9.6	13.8	11.4	5.9	14.2	15.9
σ	2.9	8.6	2.2	3.9	2.7	2.3	2.9	2.7	1.9	1.4	2.7	3.7

From Zaccaria and Weir (1967)

Figure 24. POI Profile for an Adult Sample Participating in an Alcoholic Treatment Program (N=70).

In this same study, using a pre- and post-test design, significant differences in discrepancy scores were found between a group having individual therapy and a group not having individual therapy. All pre- and post-test score changes for the therapy group were in the direction of greater self-actualizing. Weir concluded by suggesting that the POI and its theoretical orientation is useful in out-patient treatment of alcoholics. Further analyses of these data suggested that the lack of significant differences between alcoholics and their spouses appears to substantiate the contention that an alcoholic problem for one family member also influences the dynamics and adjustment of the spouse.

In examining differences between adolescents from Catholic families with alcohol problems as contrasted with those from Catholic families without such problems, Kammeier (1971) found few significant differences. Only one POI subscale (Self-Actualizing Value) reached significance at the .05 confidence level. Kammeier concluded that the misuse of alcohol by the parents in this study did not appear to be a direct cause of severe problems of maladjustment among adolescent members of the family.

POI scores from a sample of recovered alcoholics who were members of Alcoholics Anonymous and sober for one year or more were compared with those from a sample of "practicing" alcoholics. All POI scales were significantly higher for the Alcoholics Anonymous sample except Nature of Man. Profiles for these samples as reported by Kremers (1974) are presented in Figure 25.

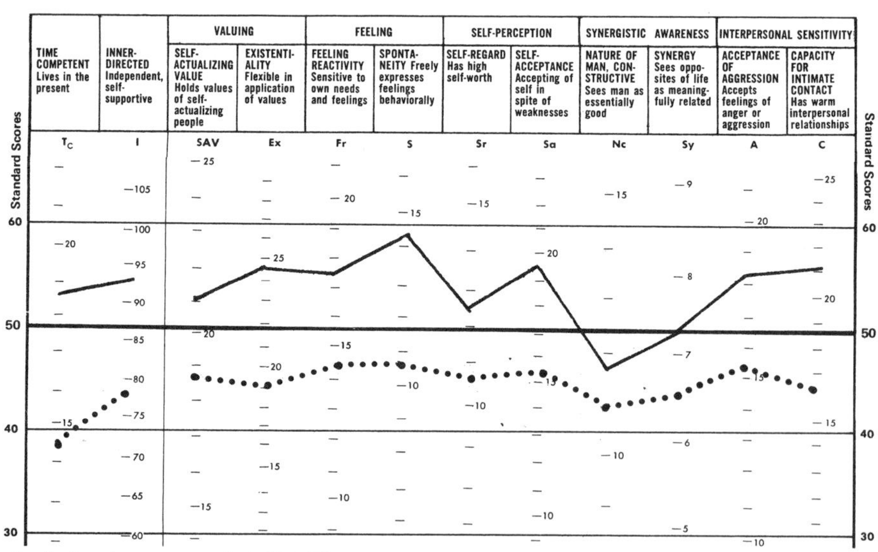

Alcoholics Anonymous (—) (N=26)

	T_C	I	SAV	Ex	Fr	S	Sr	Sa	Nc	Sy	A	C
m	18.7	93.5	21.0	24.6	17.4	14.1	12.5	19.2	11.8	7.2	18.1	21.0
σ	1.9	7.9	2.8	3.3	2.7	2.1	1.9	3.3	1.7	.8	2.1	3.3

Practicing Alcoholics (- - -) (N=24)

	T_C	I	SAV	Ex	Fr	S	Sr	Sa	Nc	Sy	A	C
m	14.4	79.1	18.7	19.0	14.3	10.7	10.8	15.2	11.0	6.5	15.1	16.2
σ	3.4	10.2	3.4	4.0	3.1	2.9	2.7	3.6	1.7	1.3	3.7	3.7

Based on data reported by Kremers (1974)

Figure 25. POI Profiles for a Sample from Alcoholics Anonymous and a Sample of Practicing Alcoholics.

Normative data based on samples of alcoholic patients tested in other settings generally follow the POI profile pattern obtained by Zaccaria and Weir (1967). Data reported by David Jansen (1974), based on a sample from Wilmar State Hospital generally parallel those reported above. (See Figure 26.) Important characteristics would appear to be a generally below-average profile, approximating that of the nominated nonactualizing sample (see Figure 3, p. 10), with markedly lower TC scores.

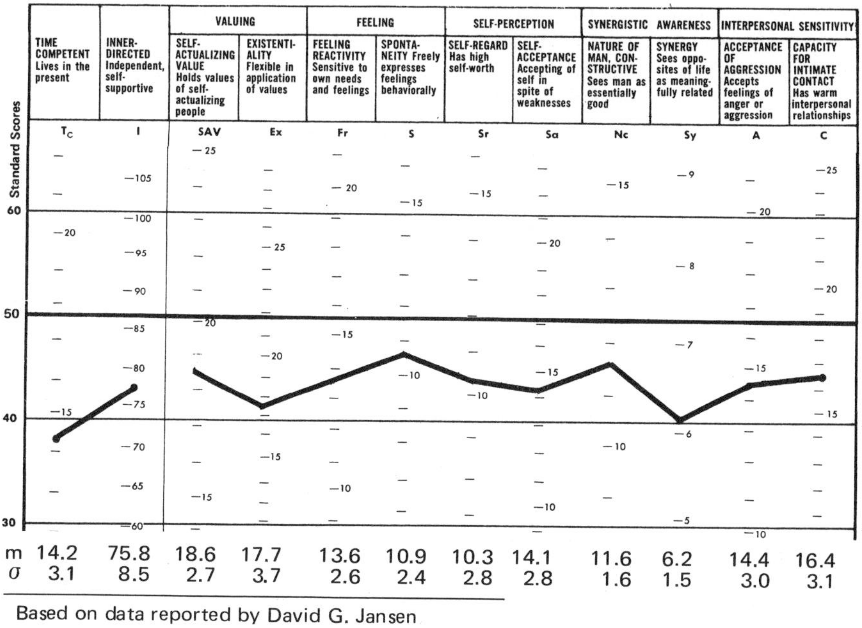

Figure 26. POI Profile for a State Hospital Sample of Male Alcoholics (N=146).

The typical alcoholic POI profile is low, generally about one standard deviation below the "normal" adult mean. Particularly low scores are reflected on Time Competence and Synergy. Low Time Competence scores seen in this as well as the drug addict, delinquent, and felon samples probably reflect the fellings of guilt and resentment about past events that led to the maladaptive behavior.

A major thrust of POI research in alcoholic treatment involves the orientation toward positive concepts of personal growth rather than the employment of a pathological frame of reference. Treatment of the alcoholic in terms of dynamics of family life and examination of the effects of alcoholism on other members of the family have been reflected in this research.

The foregoing studies are typical of a trend that regards emotional health as a series of points along a continuum, the lower end of which is marked by psychopathology and the upper end by actualizing. Heretofore, the approach has been to inquire of the person manifesting some form of abnormal behavior, "How sick are you?" Clearly, since the early 1960s, when E.M. Jellinek (1960) and others introduced the "disease concept of alcoholism," many investigators tended to use measures of abnormality such as the Rorschach, and various questionnaires, notably the MMPI, to obtain an answer to this question. Eysenck (1971) and others have emphasized the genetic contribution to acute alcoholism. However, as alcoholics move from a position in which their behavior is basically controlled by physiological demands for the drug (a biomedical problem) to one in which, through abstinence, they are again able to return to a comparatively normal existence, they are in a position to assume control over the development of their own selfhood; to be amenable to the educational precepts involved in actualizing (an educational problem). Because everyone has attained some degree of emotional growth and maturation, it is becoming increasingly more to the point to inquire of the recovered alcoholic, "How well are you?" where "wellness" is a measure of actualizing. At this point, researchers are in a position to pay more attention to the positive aspects of mental health and to avoid the label of "pathological" until it can with some tangible justification be applied. The emphasis placed on actualizing as an educational process, as distinct from the more traditional medical approach, has clearly been delineated by Shostrom et al. (1976) and is reflected in alcoholism research using the POI.

This approach has one significant advantage: It begins with a positive position of health rather than the negative one of illness. In testing the various aspects of healthy maturing and actualizing, as evinced by the extent to which the person is fully functioning and tends to be self-oriented and, indeed, regards fellow humans with trust and tolerance, the POI, again and again, is proving its effectiveness. Alcoholics, confused and beset with addictive compulsions though they may be, do possess some stature as regards their own emotional development. Where the areas of positive growth may be, and to what extent they have been realized, is what the POI is able to signify. This is most important for the alcoholism counselor, since it is upon these strengths that he or she can begin building in bringing the client to a more meaningful rehabilitation. Alcoholism counseling is a special discipline that requires a "feel" for just the proper places to apply the therapeutic thrust, so as to encourage alcoholics and to alter their attitudes toward themselves and their environment, including family setting. The POI has proven itself to be valuable in assisting the counselor in halting the downward decline of alcoholics and in promoting their upward climb to increasing self-respect and self-acceptance, so essential to their recovery and subsequent well-being.

Drug Abuse

The POI has been used in a number of settings relating self-actualizing to drug use. That concepts measured by the POI are relevant to problems of drug abuse has been demonstrated in a study by Oas (1971). In a sample of 719 junior- and senior-high-school students, an investigation was undertaken to determine the relationship between students, self-reported use of drugs and POI measurements concerning their expressing or receiving affection and anger. Seventy-two drug users were identified from the sample, 185 were identified as drug experimenters, forty-four as marijuana users only, thirty-six as moderate users, and 382 as never having used unprescribed drugs. Another sample of twenty-one students who had been expelled for drug use was identified. Analyses of POI scores indicated that those males expelled for drug use were significantly lower in expressing or receiving affection, as indicated by the POI Capacity for Intimate Contact scale, than were those males who were drug users but who were not expelled, or those males who experimented with drugs. However, females who were drug users (including those expelled) evidenced more positive expressing and receiving of affection than those who had never used drugs, who had only experimented with drugs, or who had used marijuana only.

With regard to their handling of anger, as measured by the POI Acceptance of Aggression scale, males who were drug users, including those who had been expelled for drug use, were significantly lower in their expressing or receiving of anger than those males who had never used drugs, used marijuana only, or were moderate users. However, females who were drug users, or who had been expelled for drug use, scored significantly higher in their expressing or receiving of anger than did those females who had never used drugs, or had experimented occasionally. The major conclusions reached by the author were that males expelled for drug use had negative response toward affectional relationships as compared to other groups and that among the drug-user and expelled samples there are significant differences between males and females in their mean scores measuring handling of affection and anger.

A number of military-sponsored drug-rehabilitation programs have incorporated the POI to assess the effects of encounter experience among drug users. Knapp and Fitzgerald (1973) reported on the use of the POI in assessing change among participants in a seventy-two hour weekend transgenerational workshop. This program, sponsored by the Bureau of Naval Personnel, was designed to establish community feeling among Navy personnel, many of whom had drug abuse problems. Since evaluation of the workshop technique was concerned with evaluation of personality changes of comparatively greater permanence, retesting was administered from one to eight months following the experience. Significant POI subscale increases were obtained for the major Inner-Directed scale as well as for the Feeling Reactivity, Spontaneity, Self-Regard, and Acceptance of Aggression subscales. Interpreting from scale descriptions, results of the workshop experience might suggest an increased sensitivity to internal needs and feelings, (Fr) increased freedom to express feelings spontaneously (S), increased affirmation of self-strengths (Sr), and increased acceptance and understanding of natural aggressiveness (A), as opposed to defensiveness and repression of these tendencies.

In a study of the effects of a drug education and counseling program for Air Force personnel, concentrating on communication laboratories that emphasized Transactional Analysis, Kaats (1972) found compelling evidence in support of the hypothesis that completion of the program would be associated with higher levels of self-actualizing. Nine of the twelve POI scales were significantly higher (.01 level) following the course.

Kilmann (1974) has reported normative data for a sample of institutionalized female narcotic addicts as shown in Figure 27. When com-

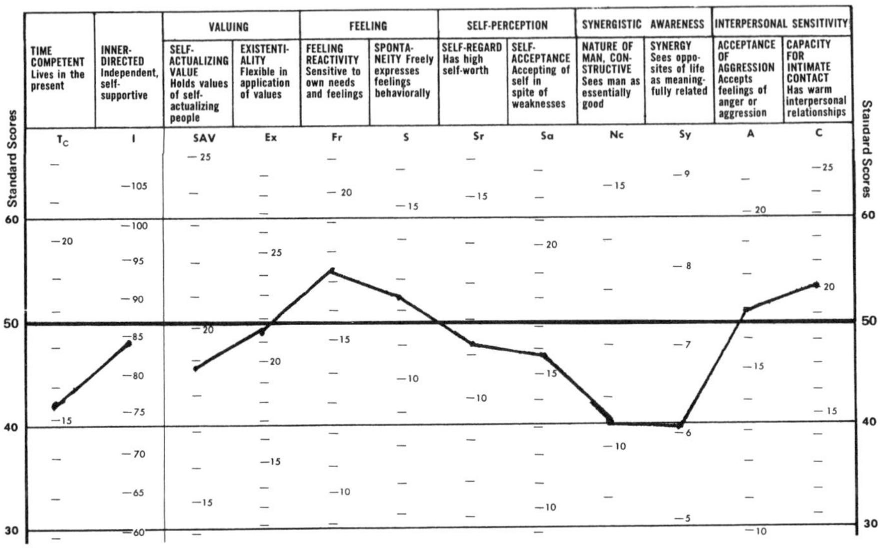

m	15.5	84.6	18.9	21.2	17.2	12.4	11.2	15.9	10.4	6.1	17.0	20.0
σ	3.5	11.5	3.4	4.2	3.0	2.5	2.9	3.1	3.0	1.7	2.8	3.4

From Kilmann (1974)

Figure 27. POI Profile for a Sample of Female Narcotic Drug Addicts (N=84).

pared to the normal adult sample, significantly lower scores were obtained for Time Competence, Self-Actualizing Value, Self-Regard, Self-Acceptance, Nature of Man, and Synergy. Interestingly, higher scores were obtained for Feeling Reactivity, Spontaneity, and Capacity for Intimate Contact. Interpreting the results in terms of the scale descriptions, Kilmann notes that in comparing obtained statistically significant differences with the normal adult sample, addicts may be described as less effective in their use of time, less satisfied with their lives and with themselves, skeptical of man's goodness, more sensitive toward their own needs and feelings, more spontaneous in expressing feelings, and better able to develop meaningful relationships with others. Kilmann suggests implications for therapeutic treatment for this population that include the reduction of personal deficiencies as determined from POI results. These include direction toward the structuring of more efficient use of time in the present and the development of self-acceptance, feelings of self-worth, and trust in other human beings. Noting the measured high sensitivity to personal needs and feelings and spontaneity in expressing feelings Kilmann states that "it logically follows that a 'here-and-now' therapist approach presented within a 'feelings-oriented' framework would be an appropriate consideration" (p. 309).

Cryns (1974) has reported the results of a study designed to assess the personality attributes of heroin addicts in a methadone maintenance program. The purpose was empirically to compare objective results from a sample of seventy addicts voluntarily committed to rehabilitation with a control sample of eleven nontreated, in terms of personality constructs stated in terms of positive or normal personality characteristics. The results, shown in Figure 28, suggest a relatively higher level of actualizing for the methadone treatment group as evidenced by significantly higher POI scores on Existentiality, Self-Regard, Self-Acceptance, and Acceptance of Aggression.

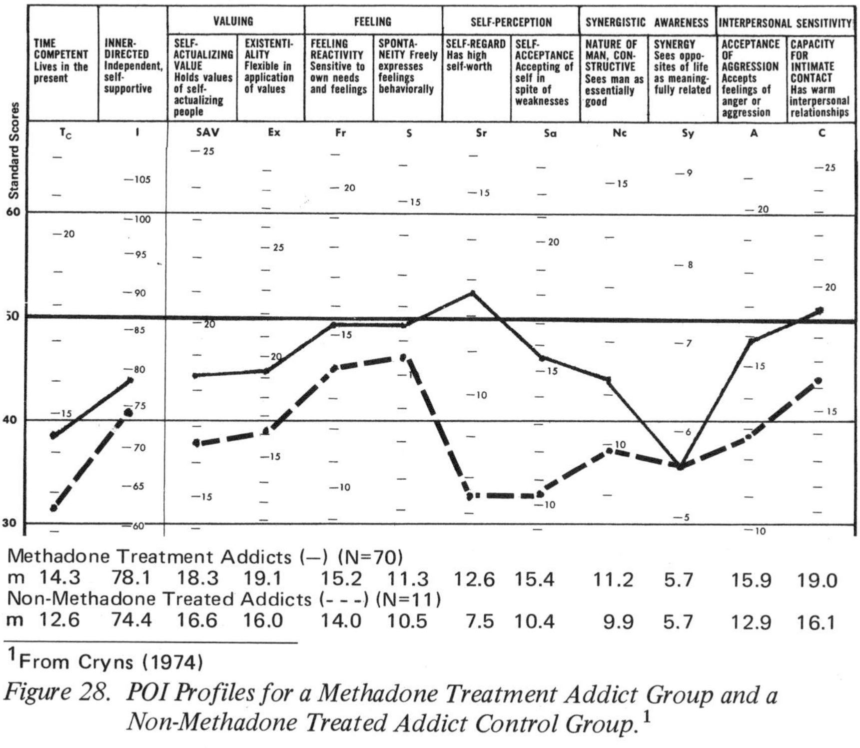

Methadone Treatment Addicts (—) (N=70)
m 14.3 78.1 18.3 19.1 15.2 11.3 12.6 15.4 11.2 5.7 15.9 19.0
Non-Methadone Treated Addicts (- - -) (N=11)
m 12.6 74.4 16.6 16.0 14.0 10.5 7.5 10.4 9.9 5.7 12.9 16.1

[1] From Cryns (1974)

Figure 28. POI Profiles for a Methadone Treatment Addict Group and a Non-Methadone Treated Addict Control Group.[1]

Multivariate tests of the three-way (sex × race × treatment) interaction fail to reach significance as well as did all two-way interactions with the exception of two out of the forty-two computed. Thus, the data suggest no real differences in personality profiles between male or female addicts or between black and white addicts, and more importantly, as Cryns notes, that duration of methadone treatment does not result in significant changes of addicts' self-perception. Another analysis indicated that the methadone-treated addicts who received psychotherapy or counseling scored higher on POI scales of Time Competence, Spontaneity, and Self-Regard than those who did not.

POI profiles based on samples of drug users very closely approximate those based on samples of alcoholics considered in the preceding section.

Particularly characteristic are the low scores on the Time Competence scale as well as on the scales measuring synergistic awareness, Nature of Man, and Synergy.

The intervention of various treatment programs, including psychotherapeutic techniques, has resulted in an increase in POI scores similar to that reported among samples from other populations.

Several recent probings, such as the San Mateo County surveys of drug abuse among high-school students and the more comprehensive study, *Drug Use in America*, described in the Second Report of the National Commission on Marijuana and Drug Use, attest to the increasing, and largely illegal, use of drugs by Americans of all ages and from every social stratum. These surveys have defined the magnitude of this social problem, but little else of an epidemiological nature has yet been initiated. The definition of underlying causes, and the institution of social intervention programs to stem this rising tide of drug abuse, to date, have not been forthcoming. Investigators using the POI, such as those mentioned above, have made significant, if unappreciated, contributions to the etiology of drug use. As Weil (1972) and others have pointed out, people take drugs for a variety of reasons, all of them traceable to the desire to be less uncomfortable with oneself, or simply to "feel better." Such a rationale implies the existence of a "holistic void," or an "existential crisis," to borrow a term from Perls, which amounts in essence to a want of growth and maturation. Put another way, such feelings emerge from a lack of self-actualizing. That this conclusion can be drawn is amply substantiated by the foregoing studies using the POI. Not only can this instrument signify the existence of an emotional problem as a deficiency of emotional health, but it has also repeatedly identified specific areas in the drug users' personalities for which, by their use of drugs, they are attempting to compensate. These data are of paramount importance to the therapists working in drug-user rehabilitation programs, since they indicate to these professionals the aspects of their clients' personalities that need to be supported and reinforced. Short of complete addiction, these efforts can, in many cases, alleviate the users' further need for the ephemeral benefits they look to the drugs to provide.

CHAPTER 3. INTERNAL STRUCTURE AND PSYCHOMETRIC CHARACTERISTICS

STUDIES OF FAKING AND RESPONSE SETS

Deliberate faking of responses is not usually a problem when the POI is used in individual counseling or therapeutic situations. However, in certain settings, and because personality inventories depend upon self-reported behavior and values, the POI is subject to conscious as well as unconscious attempts to fake responses. The job applicant, for example, attempting to present a good image, may fake responses to certain personality items. The effects of attempts to alter the outcome of self-report inventories may be examined through a number of research designs. One such method is to ask selected samples to fake the inventory in a particular way.

In an early study with college students, reported in the POI Manual (Shostrom, 1974), Knapp administered the POI to beginning psychology students with instructions to respond as though they were applying for a job and wanted to make a good impression. The instructions were:

> This is an experiment to determine the effects of certain response sets on questionnaires. You are asked to answer the questionnaire as though you wanted to make a good impression of yourself. You should answer as though you were applying for a job and wanted to make the most favorable impression of yourself. Remember, the object is to make a good impression. (p. 20)

Profiles based on standard and "fake good" instructions are presented in Figure 29. When results of the "good impression" set were compared with scores of another sample of introductory psychology students at the same college, obtained differences, in general, were not in the direction of greater self-actualizing. Furthermore, except for the two subscales of Self-Regard and Nature of Man-Constructive, the profile based on mean scores obtained under these conditions did not reach the "normal adult" norms presented with the Inventory. The mean score for the Existentiality subscale was

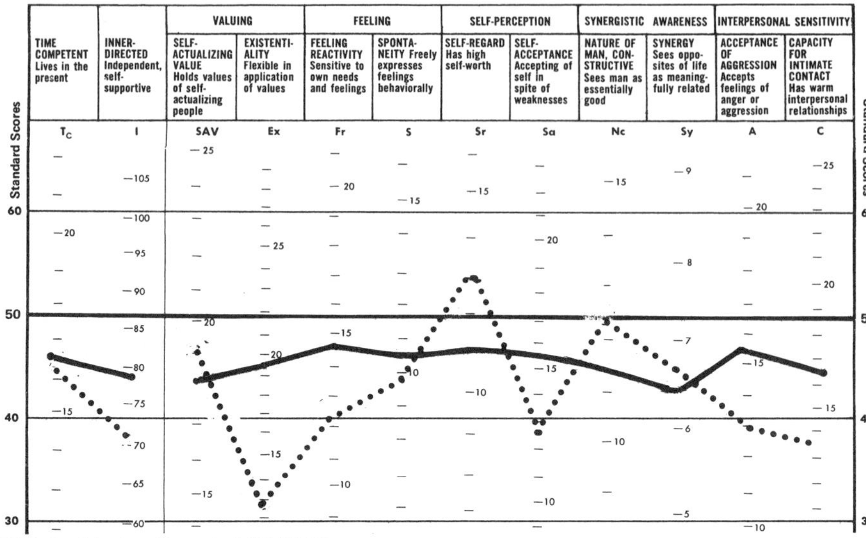

Standard Instructions (—) (N=136)

	Tc	I	SAV	Ex	Fr	S	Sr	Sa	Nc	Sy	A	C
m	16.3	79.2	18.3	19.5	14.7	10.4	11.0	15.5	11.6	6.4	15.6	16.6
σ	2.8	9.7	2.8	3.7	2.8	2.6	2.6	3.2	2.0	1.4	3.2	3.4

"Fake Good" (- - -) (N=86)

	Tc	I	SAV	Ex	Fr	S	Sr	Sa	Nc	Sy	A	C
m	16.2	70.7	19.0	12.4	12.1	9.8	13.0	12.6	12.4	6.7	13.0	13.7
σ	2.7	9.6	2.8	3.3	3.0	2.3	1.9	3.1	1.8	1.4	3.2	3.1

Based on data reported by Knapp (Shostrom, 1974)

Figure 29. POI Profiles Based on Standard and "Fake Good" Instructions for College Student Samples.

markedly distorted (over one standard deviation) *away* from the self-actualizing pole and in the direction of emphasis on rigid adherence to traditional values. Since instructions were to make a favorable impression for employment purposes, it may be that college students perceive the individual who rigidly adheres to rules and principles as a better organization man, compulsively fulfilling all obligations. It is interesting to note that of the several executive and upper-management samples for which POI scores have been reported, the Existentiality subscale is markedly lower than those reported for samples of individuals in counseling, teaching, or other occupations in the liberal arts or humanities. While not distorting their scores in the direction of the self-actualizing individuals reflected by higher POI scores, perhaps the college sample is accurately gauging the direction of response distortion. The distortion, however, was much greater than appropriate, moving the "good impression" mean further below empirically obtained managerial means than typical college profiles are above. Other marked changes produced by the "good impression" set were higher Self-Regard scores and lower Self-Acceptance scores.

In a subsequent replication of this study, Foulds and Warehime (1971a) found much the same pattern. Profiles for this sample are presented in Figure 30. The authors concluded that deliberate attempts by undergraduate college students to "fake good" do not produce profiles

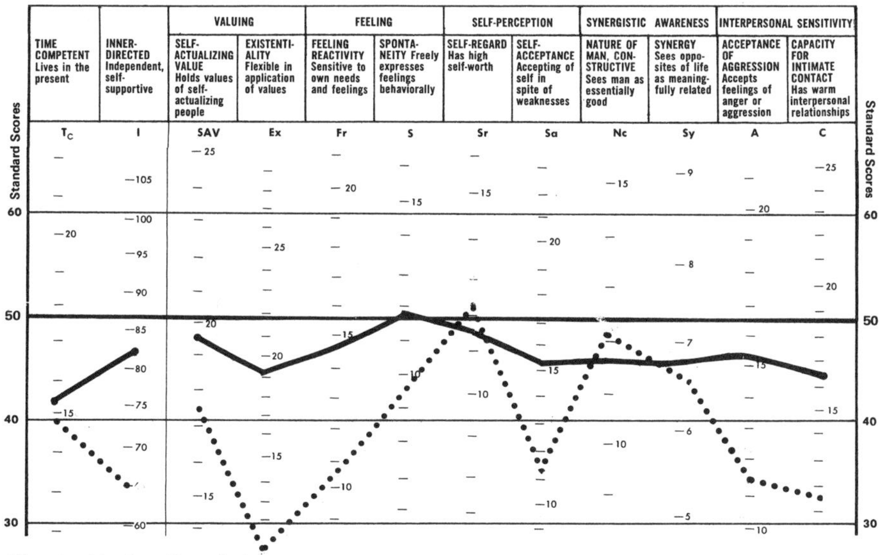

	Tc	I	SAV	Ex	Fr	S	Sr	Sa	Nc	Sy	A	C
Standard Instructions (—)												
m	15.5	80.8	19.4	19.2	14.7	11.9	11.7	15.2	11.7	6.8	15.6	16.4
σ	3.2	9.3	2.5	4.2	3.1	2.6	2.1	3.2	1.8	1.2	3.0	3.5
"Fake Good" (- - -)												
m	14.9	65.0	17.4	10.6	10.4	9.5	12.4	11.3	12.1	6.7	11.4	11.7
σ	2.7	10.7	2.9	3.7	2.9	2.3	1.9	3.6	1.8	1.3	3.2	3.3

From Foulds and Wareheim (1971)

Figure 30. POI Profiles Based on Standard and "Fake Good" Instructions (N=95).

characteristic of self-actualizing individuals and that students' conceptions of the "well-adjusted person" in our society are not entirely congruent with the model of the "self-actualizing person" followed in development of the POI. The authors suggest that their findings provide increased confidence in the results obtained from use of the POI with college students.

In a study of the effects of "ideal self" instructions, Braun and Asta (1969) also found results inconsistent across the POI scales. On six scales subjects appeared more self-actualizing under ideal-self instructions than under standard instructions, while on four others the reverse was true. Inner-Directedness and Capacity for Intimate Contact were not affected significantly by the different instructions.

In studying the responses of felons to the POI, Fisher (1968) found, in a sample of 150, that this group scores significantly lower than normal subjects on eight of twelve POI scales. When instructed to make a good impression, felons achieved lower scores on nine of the twelve scales, which Fisher (1973) interpreted to mean that felons conceive of society as endorsing a lesser degree of self-actualizing than that which they themselves possess. Following up these findings, Fisher and Silverstein (1969a) then administered the POI to two felon samples, one a control sample and the other with instructions to simulate poor adjustment. Lower scores on eight scales and a higher score on one subscale, Existentiality, were obtained under the "poor adjustment" instructions. The authors conclude that felons do recognize the social acceptability of the self-actualizing concept but possess a distorted view of the norm, feeling that they are more self-actualizing than is normal or socially acceptable in the culture. As in the case of the college student samples, it is interesting to note the divergent shifting of scales, particularly the Existentiality subscale, under faking instructions.

Following a series of studies into "fakability" of the POI (Braun, 1966, 1969), which resulted in profiles similar to those obtained in the studies described above, Braun and LaFaro (1969) concluded that the lower scores resulting from attempts to make a good impression or appear well-adjusted on the POI demonstrate an "unexpected resistance to faking," making the instrument "unique among self-report instruments."

In the first of these studies, Braun (1966) administered the POI with instructions to answer as would a "typical neurotic"; then, upon an immediate second administration, as this same hypothetical person would answer after two years of therapy. On all twelve POI scales appreciably more favorable scores were achieved with the "after therapy" set. In a follow-up study, Braun and LaFaro (1969) administered the POI to four college-student groups under standard instructions, followed by readministration with instructions to either "make a good impression" or appear "well adjusted." In addition, two groups received special instruction on what self-actualizing is supposed to entail. Faked administration scores for the four groups were consistently less favorable than under standard instructions, while the two groups receiving information about the concept of the actualizing person achieved considerably more favorable scores. Braun and LaFaro concluded that "unless subjects have special information about the POI and self-actualization, the inventory shows an unexpected resistance to faking."

Based on clinical experience with the POI, and amplifying these findings, Shostrom (1973a) observed:

> From a clinical standpoint, the POI has a 'lie score profile' which can be identified easily. Since 'actualizing' persons score between T standard scores of 50 and 60, those with excessively high profiles (all T scores of 60-70) may be interpreted as 'over-enthusiastic' attempts to take the test in accordance with 'rightness' from reading Maslow and other humanistic literature. Even Maslow, himself, scored between the 50-60 T score range! (p. 480)

Resulting effects of the two major concepts of response distortion may be summarized in Figure 31. "Faking," or the conscious attempt to present oneself in a favorable (socially desirable) light, results in a generally depressed POI profile, while intellectualized responses based on a knowledge of the underlying theoretical concepts result in a typically hyperelevated profile.

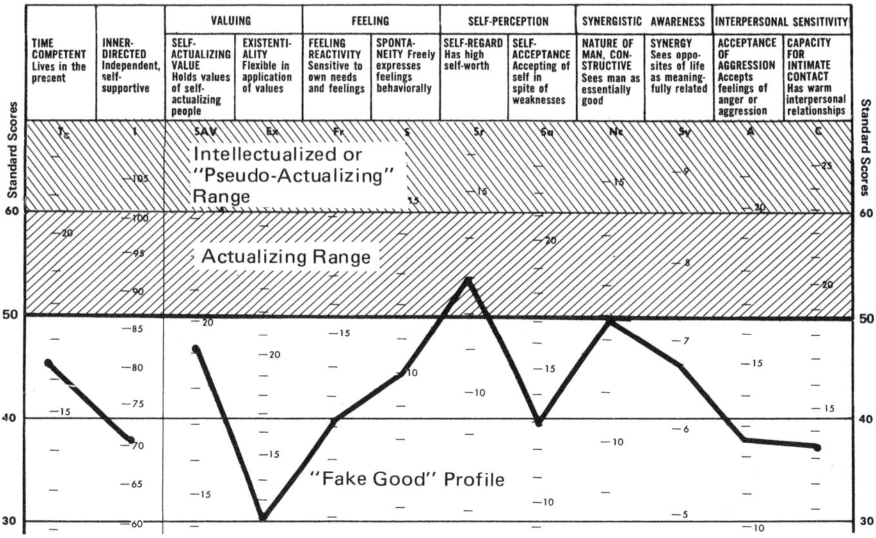

Figure 31. POI "Fake Good" Profile Plotted Against Actualizing and Pseudo-Actualizing Score Ranges.

It is interesting to speculate upon possible reasons for this discrepancy between actual responses of self-actualizing persons and the distorted responses of those attempting to present themsleves as actualizing.

Many personality scales are keyed in the direction of generally accepted cultural standards. Development of the POI, however, was based on logical keying supported by an empirical demonstration of validity. Keying of the POI is based on the direction of the self-actualizing model of personality rather than on cultural norms. To the extent that values and behaviors defining self-actualizing differ from those of currently accepted cultural standards, POI scores may be expected to deviate under extreme motivational conditions.

An earlier study by Grater (1968) and the study by Braun and LaFaro (1969) described above suggest that knowledge of the characteristics of self-actualizing persons as defined by the POI, in addition to the motivation to make a good impression, are necessary in order for individuals to distort their POI responses appreciably in the direction of self-actualizing persons. Warehime and Foulds (1973) have presented data supporting this hypothesis. In their study, POI scale scores were correlated with scores from a scale developed to measure the tendency to give socially desirable responses. Their results indicated that individuals who would tend to be successful in dissimulating scores in other evaluation situations were not successful in obtaining higher POI scores. The magnitude of correlations were interpreted as indicating those concepts wherein the self-actualizing model and cultural standards are most widely at variance.

Particularly high relationships were obtained against the Acceptance of Aggression scale.Cultural standards regarding recognition and verbal expression of aggressive feelings ("play it cool") were interpreted as being quite different from behavior sanctioned by self-actualizers. Other significant relationships were obtained against the Existentiality scale, which measures flexibility in the application of values and reduced compulsiveness and dogmatism as well as increased ability to react without blind or rigid adherence to principles.

Results of a study by Knapp and Comrey (1973) corroborate these findings. When correlated against a measure of tendency to answer in a socially acceptable way, the Response Bias (R) scale of the Comrey Personality Scales (Comrey, 1970), POI scales of Inner-Directed, Existentiality, Feeling Reactivity, Self-Acceptance, Acceptance of Aggression, and Capacity for Intimate Contact were all significantly and negatively correlated.

Thus the person who truly accepts and lives by the statements "I do not always tell the truth," "I do not always need to live by the rules and standards of society," and "I do not feel obligated when a stranger does me a favor" may in fact be more self-actualizing but, when asked to give the favorable answer, might respond "I feel I must always tell the truth," "I live by the rules and standards of society," and "I feel obligated when a stranger does me a favor."

In a series of studies in which college students were presented either information about the concept of self-actualizing, information about more conventional social adjustment, or no information, Warehime, Routh, and Foulds (1974) found that those receiving information about the concept of self-actualizing were able to increase their scores on the POI when asked to use this information. However, when asked to respond honestly their scores were unaffected by such knowledge. Furthermore, scores on a social desirability scale were not related to the tendency of subjects to dissimulate POI responses. The authors concluded that the Inner-Directed scale is more resistant to faking than many other self-report inventories and that the POI is "remarkably unsusceptible to dissimulation."

In summary, two characteristic "lie profiles" are built into the POI that are easily detected by those trained in evaluation of the instrument. One results in a representative profile in the case of deliberate attempts to present a favorable impression without specific knowledge of concepts of actualizing. Particularly characteristic of such profiles are extremely elevated Self-Regard scores coupled with depressed Self-Acceptance and Existentiality scores. The other is a uniformly hyperelevated profile. However, in this case, following the evidence of Warehime, Routh, and Foulds (1974), when instructed to respond honestly scores may be unaffected by such knowledge.

It is felt that such "lie profile" interpretation is an even more significant technique than use of a simple "lie score," as presented in many other instruments.

Correlations with Distortion Scales and Measures of Social Desirability

Correlations of POI scores with "lie," or response distortion, scales have generally been nonsignificant. In a study by Knapp (1965) relating the POI and the *Eysenck Personality Inventory* (EPI) (Eysenck & Eysenck, 1963), very low-order correlations were found between POI scales and the EPI Lie scale. Similarly, in a study (Shostrom & Knapp, 1966) relating the POI to the MMPI (Hathaway & McKinley, 1951), no POI scale was found to be significantly correlated with the MMPI L scale, the highest *r* being .26.

Recently published data relating POI scales to measures of social desirability, however, provide further evidence concerning the relationship between present cultural definitions and standards and the self-actualizing model.

As cited above, Knapp and Comrey (1973) related POI scores among a college student sample to major personality dimensions as measured by the *Comrey Personality Scales* (CPS) (Comrey, 1970). Correlations in that study were also obtained against the CPS Response Bias (R) scale, a measure of tendency to answer in a socially desirable way. All correlations were negative except that against the Nature of Man-Constructive subscale. Six of the correlations were significant beyond the .01 confidence level: those between R and Inner-Directed (r = -.34), Existentiality (r = -.51), Feeling Reactivity (r = -.30), Self-Acceptance (r = -.30), Acceptance of Aggression (r = -.31), and Capacity for Intimate Contact (r = -.40). Results of this study were held to be consistent with the theoretical writings of Maslow that self-actualizing individuals would not feel constrained to answer questions in a socially desirable direction. Further, they are consistent with earlier results of attempts to fake wherein instructions to "fake good" resulted in lower POI scores, with differences being greatest on the Existentiality subscale. In particular, Existentiality, defined in the POI as the ability to react situationally without strong, rigid adherence to principles, represents a concept that apparently is not considered socially desirable in our society.

Pursuing the social desirability issue, Abbott and Harris (1973) report "that about 28 percent of the variance in Time Competence scale scores and 10 percent of the variance in the Inner-Directed scale are confounded with the tendency to respond to the social desirability of the items" (p. 429). The extent to which such confounding may be effecting the discriminant validity of the POI is open to conjecture.

Warehime and Foulds (1973) correlated the POI with the Marlowe-Crowne Social Desirability scale (Crowne & Marlowe, 1960) and the Edwards Social Desirability scale (Edwards, 1959) in a college-student sample. The Marlowe-Crowne scale was constructed to be relatively free of statements implying psychopathology. Only three POI subscales were significantly and negatively related to the Marlowe-Crowne scale: Existentiality (r = -.31), Feeling Reactivity (r = -.21), and Acceptance of Aggression (r = -.28). The authors suggest that these may be areas wherein the self-actualizing model and cultural standards reach their greatest divergence. That the POI is more resistant to faking than other inventories may reflect the fact that the POI is keyed to the self-actualizing model rather than the cultural standards. Thus, as Warehime and Foulds conclude, social desirability scales may be of little use in assessing the fakability of inventories such as the POI.

RELIABILITY

Development of the POI is based on concepts of dynamic traits of personality, thus making traditional concepts of reliability inappropriate in many instances. This is particularly true in the case of estimates of stability based on repeated administration over given periods of time. That the POI is highly sensitive to experiences during the interval between administrations is amply demonstrated by data presented in the section on the effects of the encounter group experience (p. 21). To some extent the rhythmical changes in personality expression central to Shostrom's theory may be expected to influence stability (test-retest) estimates for the POI. Indeed the POI is very sensitive to such changes. As Bloxom (1972) notes:

> The reliability coefficients range from a moderate .55 to a good .85. Only three subscales have coefficients that might be regarded as substandard (say, less than .70): A (.55), Nc (.66), and FR (.69). The A and Fr scales measure variables that are affect-related and, as such, may be measuring fluctuation in mood states from test to retest. (p. 291)

With this precautionary note in mind, it may be instructive to examine available studies of the stability of POI scores.

A study bearing on the test-retest reliability of the POI is that of Klavetter and Mogar (1967), who administered the POI twice, with a one-week interval, to a sample of forty-eight college students. All correlations ranged from .52 to .82. The major POI scales of Time Competence and Inner-direction displayed generally high reliability coefficients of .71 and .77 respectively. Klavetter and Mogar concluded that, with the exception of three subscales, "stability coefficients are generally high, ranging from .71 to .85" (p. 423).

Examining the stability of POI scores among a sample of forty-six student nurses over a one-year period, Ilardi and May (1968) report coefficients ranging from .32 to .74. In contrasting results of their study with those for other personality inventories administered to similar samples and approximating the same time interval, the authors conclude: "*The findings reported on the POI are well within these ranges of somewhat comparable MMPI and EPPS test-retest reliability studies*" (p. 71).

Based on readministration of the POI following a two-week interval to a sample of 172 university students, Wise and Davis (1975) report test-retest coefficients of .75 and .88 for the Time Competence and Inner-Directed scales respectively.

An interesting example of stability of POI scales in terms of transferability from sample to sample within a given occupational group is found in data reported by Lafferty (1969). Among samples to which the POI was administered, three were those of supermarket managers from three different sections of the country. Consistency of the obtained profiles can be seen in Figure 32.

Another form of reliability sometimes referred to involves the internal consistency of scales. Bloxom (1972), in reviewing the POI, suggested that

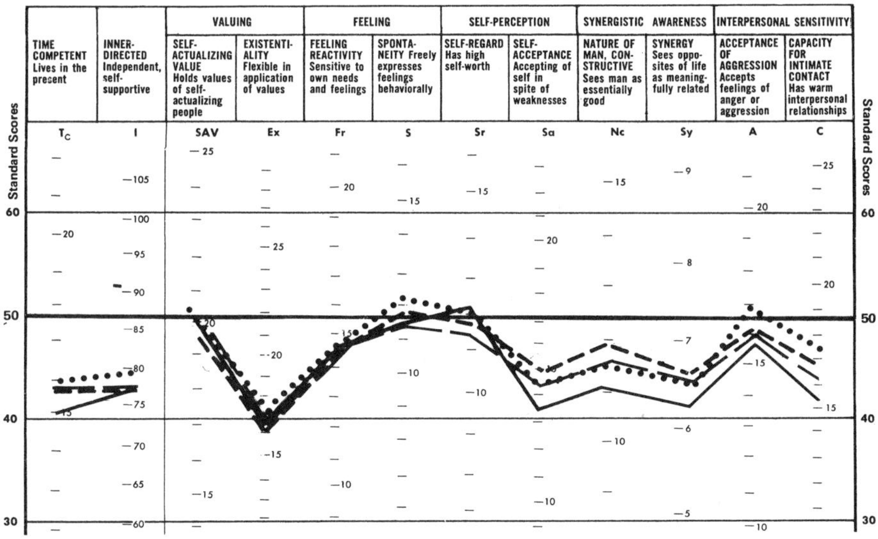

	Tc	I	SAV	Ex	Fr	S	Sr	Sa	Nc	Sy	A	C
Supermarket Managers (Chicago) (—) (N=76)												
m	15.0	76.9	20.1	16.3	14.4	11.4	12.1	13.7	11.2	6.2	15.5	15.8
σ	3.2	10.5	2.9	4.4	2.6	2.3	2.4	3.5	2.0	1.7	3.4	3.9
Supermarket Managers (Newark) (- - -) (N=86)												
m	15.7	76.6	19.6	16.4	14.7	11.8	11.8	15.0	11.8	6.7	16.0	16.9
σ	3.3	11.2	3.0	4.5	2.8	2.2	2.2	11.1	1.7	1.3	3.1	3.8
Supermarket Managers (Houston) (—) (N=83)												
m	16.0	79.3	20.4	17.1	14.7	12.0	12.0	14.7	11.6	6.7	16.7	17.2
σ	3.1	10.1	2.5	4.3	2.9	2.3	1.9	3.0	1.8	1.3	2.7	3.5
Supermarket Managers (Williamsburg) (- - -) (N=95)												
m	15.3	77.2	19.5	16.3	14.4	11.4	11.5	14.3	11.3	6.4	15.7	16.5
σ	2.8	8.0	2.5	3.7	2.3	2.1	2.1	3.3	1.7	1.3	2.7	3.2

Figure 32. POI Profiles for Supermarket Managers and Supervisory Personnel.

because the scales use a broad range of content, indices of internal consistency should be presented. Since his review, Kaats (1973) has reported internal consistency coefficients based on Cronbach's alpha of .80 for the Inner-Directed scale and .65 for the Time Competence scale. Bloxom further notes the variables assessed are broadly defined. In this sense Cattell (1972, pp. 180-181) has suggested that in personality scale construction the ideal homogeneity is *not* the greatest attainable but an optimum low value with scale construction based on a combination of psychometric considerations. In this light the demand that items for a trait should bunch in the highest possible mutual intercorrelation confounds the surface trait (cluster) with the source trait (factor) concept. Thus, taken to its logical extreme, maximum homogeneity leads statistically to a scale with only two scores (all + or all -) and no useful range, and leads psychologically to the generation of what Tsujioka and Cattell (1964) have termed a "bloated specific" factor piled on top of the truly required broad general factor. More will be said on this topic in the section on Factorial Studies.

OVERALL MEASURES OF SELF-ACTUALIZING

Of interest for certain research purposes is a single overall estimate of level of self-actualizing as reflected in the POI. It has been suggested in the POI Manual (Shostrom, 1974, p. 6) that a quick estimate of an individual's level of actualizing may be obtained by scoring only the Time Competence and Inner-Directed scales. In another study (Knapp, 1965), the Inner-Directed scale was used as the best single estimate of self-actualizing and, in several investigations, the Inner-Directed and Time Competence scales have been the major scales used in the analysis of results.

In a study designed to evaluate various methods of combining POI scores to form an overall measure of self-actualizing among a sample of 208 high-school students, Damm (1969) compared intercorrelations between several weighted indices and POI scales to determine the relative effectiveness of these methods. The highest average correlation between the overall indices studied and POI scales was obtained by using a simple combination of raw scores from the Inner-Directed and Time Competence scales. No significant increase in predictability was obtained by converting raw score data to standard scores before combining scales. The study was later replicated (Damm, 1972) using a total sample of 656, including college students and student nurses, and confirmed the earlier conclusion that a simple combination of Inner-Directed and Time Competence raw scores was the best predictor of an overall measure of the POI and, further, that the finding could be generalized beyond adolescent samples and held equally for males and females.

Beyond the comparatively simple task of isolating the single best estimate of self-actualizing lie the tasks of empirical verification of the conceptually distinct dimensions of actualizing, alluded to in the following section dealing with interrelationships among the scales (p. 86).

CORRELATIONAL STUDIES

A number of studies have been undertaken to examine the relationship of POI variables to other personality constructs and scales. Relationship of the POI to certain clinical instruments such as the MMPI has been considered in the section on Individual Therapy and Clinical Studies.

Although developed from a very different theoretical and technical viewpoint, it will be of interest to some to examine the relationship of the POI to the major factorial trait personality inventories. Among the major taxonomies considered below are those of Cattell, Comrey, Eysenck, and Guilford.

Correlations Against Personality Factor Dimensions

The POI and the *Eysenck Personality Inventory* or EPI (Eysenck & Eysenck, 1963) were administered by Knapp (1965) to a college sample to examine relationships between these conceptually different theories of personality. Results indicated that, though developed from different theoretical viewpoints, both instruments were related to a common core of mental health. The EPI dimension of Neuroticism-Stability was negatively correlated with all POI scales, demonstrating self-actualizing is related to (although not identical with) the lack of neurotic tendencies and symptoms. The correlation of highest magnitude was -.57 against the POI scale of Time Competence, the major scale measuring orientation to the present as contrasted with orientation to the "past" (guilts) or "future" (anxiety). Negative correlations between measures of self-actualizing and the neuroticism, or emotionality, construct are supportive of Maslow's contention that he was describing mentally healthy people. POI correlations against the EPI Extraversion scale were generally positive but of a much lower magnitude, ranging up to a significant .39 against the POI Spontaneity subscale.

In a study relating POI variables to the *Guilford-Zimmerman Temperament Survey* (Guilford & Zimmerman, 1949) and to the *Sixteen Personality Factor Questionnaire* (Cattell & Eber, 1957), Meredith (1967) reported correlations ranging in magnitude up to .48, this between the G-Z Sociability (S) and the POI Self-Regard subscale. Correlations with the 16PF ranged in magnitude up to .44, this between Venturesome (H) and Self-Regard (Sr). Correlations of POI scales with the EPI, G-Z Temperament Survey and the 16PF are presented in Table 4. Considering the major POI scale of Inner-Directed, significant correlations against 16PF scales depict the self-actualizing students as active, ascendant, sociable, emotionally stable, and objective. Correlations between the other major POI scale, Time Competence, and G-Z and 16PF temperament scales, suggest that those whose primary orientation is in the present would be described (from the 16PF) as assertive, happy-go-lucky, venturesome, trusting, and self-assured; and (from the G-Z) as relaxed, active, ascendant, sociable, emotionally stable, objective, and tolerant. The relatively low magnitude of correlations between these instruments and the POI indicate that they are measuring somewhat different aspects of personality.

To examine the relationship of self-actualizing to the major personality constructs defined through factor analysis, Knapp and Comrey (1973) administered the POI and the *Comrey Personality Scales* or CPS (Comrey, 1970) to a sample of eighty-four volunteer undergraduate students. The intercorrelations are presented in Table 5. Previous findings that actualizingis related to emotional stability were reconfirmed, and certain theoretical concepts of the actualizing model as measured by the POI were shown to be meaningfully related to factorial dimensions defined in Comrey's taxonomy of personality. In particular, significant correlations of the major POI Time

TABLE 4

Correlations of Personal Orientation Inventory Scales Against the Sixteen Personality Factor Questionnaire, the Guilford-Zimmerman Temperament Survey[1] and the Eysenck Personality Inventory[2]

	Sixteen Personality Factor Questionnaire																G–Z Temperament Survey										EPI	
POI	A	B	C	E	F	G	H	I	L	M	N	O	Q_1	Q_2	Q_3	Q_4	G	R	A	S	E	O	F	T	P	M	E	N
TC	11	16	17	30*	26*	02	29*	04	-31*	02	09	-30*	13	08	10	-29*	21*	-03	22*	30*	40*	30*	11	-08	22*	08	-57*	11
I	09	05	19	42*	32*	-24*	39*	04	-14	05	03	-29*	14	-08	-04	-15	33*	-17	45*	33*	24*	25*	-02	01	05	12	-35*	33*
SAV	15	10	15	31*	22*	00	40*	02	-12	-07	00	-17	13	-12	03	-12	44*	-10	33*	36*	24*	08	-07	16	05	03	-27*	18
Ex	-05	-10	06	29*	24*	-39*	13	06	-06	02	03	-18	05	03	-15	-05	12	-25*	11	12	07	16	00	-12	04	06	-11	30*
Fr	-05	-01	11	30*	18	-10	17	-01	-02	05	00	-15	10	-07	-03	02	15	-07	34*	11	04	06	-18	11	-05	15	-08	30*
S	07	03	17	35*	33*	-23*	38*	-01	-08	02	06	-23*	13	-16	-11	-10	32*	-19	40*	32*	11	14	-02	-01	00	12	-34*	39*
Sr	13	14	36*	30*	23*	09	44*	-05	-28*	-12	12	-36*	11	-12	24*	-33*	38*	01	45*	48*	43*	31*	01	02	09	23*	-52*	36*
Sa	13	03	12	24*	25*	-18	22*	08	-12	10	06	-19	06	00	-01	-09	08	-11	25*	25*	12	16	07	-05	05	-04	-17	10
Nc	12	16	18	00	08	-06	05	13	-26*	-14	03	-21*	10	-03	09	-13	16	12	14	08	20	23*	18	03	26*	01	-21	-05
Sy	09	13	14	19	17	-10	20	-07	-07	-06	05	-16	08	-07	-06	-03	33*	-02	14	19	17	15	16	18	07	12	-25	06
A	01	-04	15	39*	24*	-08	30*	-12	04	04	03	-08	04	-11	-08	07	24*	-10	45*	28*	13	15	-14	07	-04	16	-09	37*
C	-05	01	08	33*	20	-20	25*	01	-06	09	01	-19	13	-03	-10	-09	13	-16	33*	23*	14	19	-04	-01	-01	14	-24	26*

[1]Based on a sample of 159 college students reported by Gerald M. Meredith (1967). Decimals omitted. *$p < .01$.

[2]Based on a sample of 94 college students reported by Knapp (1965).

TABLE 5

Correlations Between the Personal Orientation Inventory and the Comrey Personality Scales[1]

	POI Scales	Comrey Personality Scales									
		V	R	T	O	C	A	S	E	M	P
TC	Time Competence	18	-16	00	-08	-27	18	50	18	17	-03
I	Inner-Directed	17	-34	-02	-30	-31	24	43	25	22	-11
SAV	Self-Actualizing Value	15	-12	16	-11	-14	39	43	29	17	13
Ex	Existentiality	05	-51	-07	-42	-36	-08	17	-04	18	-31
Fr	Feeling Reactivity	06	-30	-17	-27	-21	08	22	20	07	-10
S	Spontaneity	17	-16	-07	-20	-20	30	37	37	14	05
Sr	Self-Regard	29	-17	01	-05	-20	38	66	41	27	-06
Sa	Self-Acceptance	13	-30	-04	-31	-20	04	37	16	16	-11
Nc	Nature of Man	-02	05	48	04	09	10	29	05	-25	20
Sy	Synergy	-04	-16	21	00	-01	23	27	24	-04	05
A	Acceptance of Aggression	14	-31	-24	-18	-20	23	26	34	31	-19
C	Capacity for Intimate Contact	16	-40	-20	-25	-36	10	31	19	20	-28

[1]Decimals omitted. Correlations above .27 are significant at the .01 confidence level and above .21 at the .05 confidence level. Based on a sample of 84 college students reported by Knapp and Comrey (1973).

Competence and Inner-Directed scales to the CPS Emotional Stability scale (r = .50 and .43 respectively) supported the hypothesis that overall estimates of self-actualizing would be positively related to stability. Other hypotheses supported by the data were confirmed by the negative relationships between actualizing, particularly in terms of the Existentiality scale and the CPS Social Conformity scale (r = -.36), and the positive correlation between the POI Nature of Man-Constructive scale and the CPS Trust versus Defensiveness (T) scale (r = .48), similarly defined as measuring a basic belief and trust in the goodness and worth of human nature.

The significant correlations between POI scales and scales representing the major factorial taxonomies of personality (as defined by Andre Comrey, Hans J. Eysenck, Raymond B. Cattell, and J.P. Guilford) are summarized in Table 6.

TABLE 6

Relationship of Self-Actualizing as Measured by the Personal Orientation Inventory to Factor Theories of Personality[1]

Shostrom (POI)	Comrey (CPS)	Eysenck (EPI)	Cattell (16PF)	Guilford (G-Z Temp)
TC Time Competence	Rebellious (C, -.27) Emotionally Stable (S, .50)	Emotionally Stable (N, -.57)	Assertive (E, .30) Happy-go-lucky (F, .26) Venturesome (H, .29) Trusting (L, -.31) Self-Assured (O, -.30) Relaxed (Q_4, -.29)	Active (G, .21) Ascendant (A, .22) Sociable (S, .30) Emotionally Stable (E, .40) Objective (O, .30) Good Personal Relations (P, .22)
I Inner-Directed	Lack of Compulsion (O, -.30) Rebellious (C -.31) Emotionally Stable (S, .43)	Extraverted (E, .33) Emotionally Stable (N, -.35)	Assertive (E, .42) Happy-go-lucky (F, .32) Expedient (G, -.24) Venturesome (H, .39) Self-Assured (O, -.29)	Active (G, .33) Ascendant (A, .45) Sociable (S, .33) Emotionally Stable (E, .24) Objective (O, .23)
SAV Self-Actualizing Values	Active (A, .39) Emotionally Stable (S, .43) Extraverted (E, .29)	Emotionally Stable (N, -.27)	Assertive (E, .31) Happy-go-lucky (F, .22) Venturesome (H, .40)	Active (G, .44) Ascendant (A, .33) Sociable (S, .36) Emotionally Stable (E, .24)
Ex Existentiality	Lack of Compulsion (O, -.42) Rebellious (C, -.36) Egocentric (P, -.31)	Extraverted (E, .30)	Assertive (E, .29) Happy-go-lucky (F, .24) Expedient (G, -.39)	Unrestrained (R, -.25)
Fr Feeling Reactivity	Lack of Compulsion (O, -.27)	Extraverted (E, .30)	Assertive (E, .30)	Ascendant (A, .34)
S Spontaneity	Active (A, .30) Emotionally Stable (S, .37) Extraverted (E, .37)	Extraverted (E, .39) Emotionally Stable (N, -.34)	Assertive (E, .35) Happy-go-lucky (F, .33) Expedient (G, -.23) Venturesome (H, .38) Self-Assured (O, -.23)	Active (G, .32) Ascendant (A, .40) Sociable (S, .32)

Sr Self-Regard	Active (A, .38) Emotionally Stable (S, .66) Extraverted (E, .41) Masculine (M, .27)	Extraverted (E, .36) Emotionally Stable (N, -.52)	Emotionally Stable (C, .36) Assertive (E, .30) Happy-go-lucky (F, .23) Venturesome (H, .44) Trusting (L, -.28) Self-Assured (O, -.36) Controlled (Q_3, .24) Relaxed (Q_4, -.33)	Active (G, .38) Ascendant (A, .45) Sociable (S, .48) Emotionally Stable (E, .43) Objective (O, .31) Masculine (M, .23)
Sa Self-Acceptance	Lack of Compulsion (O, -.31) Emotionally Stable (S, .29)		Assertive (E, .24) Happy-go-lucky (F, .25) Venturesome (H, .22)	Ascendant (A, .25) Sociable (S, .25)
Nc Nature of Man – Constructive	Trusting (E, .48) Emotionally Stable (S, .29)		Trusting (L, -.26) Self-Assured (O, -.21)	Objective (O, .23) Good Personal Relations (P, .26)
Sy Synergy	Emotionally Stable (S, .27)			Active (G, .33)
A Acceptance of Aggression	Extraverted (E, .34) Masculine (M, .31)	Extraverted (E, .37)	Assertive (E, .39) Happy-go-lucky (F, .24) Venturesome (H, .30)	Active (G, .24) Ascendant (A, .45) Sociable (S, .28)
C Capacity for Intimate Contact	Rebellious (C, -.36) Emotionally Stable (S, .31) Egocentric (P, -.28)	Extraverted (E, .26)	Assertive (E, .33) Venturesome (H, .25)	Ascendant (A, .33) Sociable (S, .23)

[1]Relationships significant at the .01 confidence level or beyond only are tabled.
Relationships against the CPS are based on data presented by Knapp and Comrey (1973); those against the EPI by Knapp (1965); and those against the 16PF, and G-Z Temp. are from data presented by Meredith (1967).
Factor titles are typed to reflect direction of relationship. Factor identification and the correlation coefficient is presented in parentheses following the title.

While these relationships will probably be of greatest usefulness to individuals familiar with one or more of the earlier instruments, in obtaining a landmark for exploration of the POI a few generalizations might be in order. Regarding conceptual overlap between the POI and the factorial instruments, the Self-Regard subscale most clearly represents the traditional emotional-stability dimension. Correlations obtained against the corresponding emotional-stability dimension were .66 for the Comrey taxonomy, .52 for Eysenck, .43 for Guilford, and .36 for Cattell.

POI subscales for which little overlapping variance appeared, with no correlation over .40 (accounting for less than 16 percent of the variance), were Feeling Reactivity, Spontaneity, Self-Acceptance, Synergy, and Capacity for Intimate Contact. These perhaps most clearly represent complex new concepts garnered from humanistic theories of personality for which further evidence of construct validity is best obtained from other, outside, sources.

Correlations Against Ipsative Inventories

In an exploratory study by Grossack, Armstrong, and Lussiev (1966), POI scales were related to the scales of the *Edwards Personal Preference Survey* (Edwards, 1959). Positive correlations were found between the major POI Inner-Directed scale and EPPS scales of Autonomy and Heterosexuality, and negative correlations between the POI Inner-Directed and the EPPS Abasement and Order scores. Extending the above study, Le May and Damm (1969) considered correlations between the POI and EPPS separately for males and females. Although, as the authors note, it is difficult to interpret results of correlations between ipsative (EPPS) and normative (POI) measures, it was of interest to note comparative differences between the sexes in terms of patterns of significant correlations against the POI. In the male sample, EPPS Autonomy and Abasement scales had relatively greater relationship to the POI. Five POI scales were significantly related to Autonomy in a positive direction and seven POI scales were negatively related to Abasement. In the female sample, four POI scales were significantly and positively related to Change and four were negatively related to Order.

Braun and Asta (1968) investigated the relationship between the POI and the *Gordon Personal Inventory* (Gordon, 1956). High, significant correlations were obtained between the GPI Personal Relations scale and the POI subscales of Nature of Man-Constructive ($r = .51$) and Self-Actualizing Value ($r = .42$). Five of the nine significant correlations were with the GPI Original Thinking scale, which, as Braun and Asta note, is consistent with the theorizing of Maslow (1962), in which the creativeness of the self-actualizing individual has been emphasized. Further, these findings are consistent with the empirical finding of Damm (1970) that POI scores among a high-school sample are significantly and positively related to scores from the *Remote Associates Test* (Mednick & Mednick, 1967).

Correlations Against Demographic Characteristics

Several studies have related POI scores to home background and other demographic variables. Gibb (1968), in relating self-actualizing to home background, found that those college students scoring comparatively higher on the POI were (1) from homes in which the parents had finished high school and had additional formal education, (2) from families with one to three children, (3) from families whose mother had worked full-time, (4) from families providing little or no formal religious training, and (5) presently not actively involved in religious participation.

La Bach (1969) found, in a college sample, that the major Inner-Directed and Time Competence scales were positively related to age, year in college, marital status, and satisfaction with college. In addition, the POI I scale was positively related to number of hours worked per week, infrequent attendance at religious services, political liberalism, and identification with an academic or nonconformist subculture.

A number of other studies have shown that individuals scoring comparatively high in terms of self-actualizing as contrasted with low scorers, tend to be more liberal in social philosophy (Gunnison, 1964), tend to express a lower need to control the behavior of their children (Swift, 1966), and tend to rank occupational values differently (Masucci, 1966).

Age-Related Trends

Evidence concerning trends in POI scores with age are available from a number of sources. From a theoretical standpoint it has been hypothesized that peaks of actualizing cannot be reached until full maturity is attained. As noted earlier, Maslow (1970) stated that in searching a college campus for self-actualizing persons, "I had to conclude that self-actualization of the sort I had found in my older subjects was not possible in our society for young developing people" (p. 150). Shostrom, Knapp, and Knapp (1976) have further developed this theoretical position.

Empirical data based on administration of the POI have supported this contention. Mean scores for adult samples tend to be higher than those based on high-school-student samples. Advanced college-student samples are higher than entering college students', and samples from both of these populations are higher than high-school student samples. Andrew Greely's (1970) data from the Catholic-Priest sample, described on p. 48, may be brought to bear on the age-trend issue. POI results from this sample were analyzed by ten-year age intervals ranging from twenty-six to thirty-five to fifty-six and over. These profiles are shown in Figure 33. In general there appears to be a tendency for POI scores to decrease with age. The correlation between age and the Inner-Directed scale was -.34.

Jansen (1974) has reported POI means for ten-year age intervals from twenty to thirty up to fifty-one to sixty for samples of state hospital alcoholics. The only significant differences obtained were in the direction of increased POI scores with age, although the changes were not of great

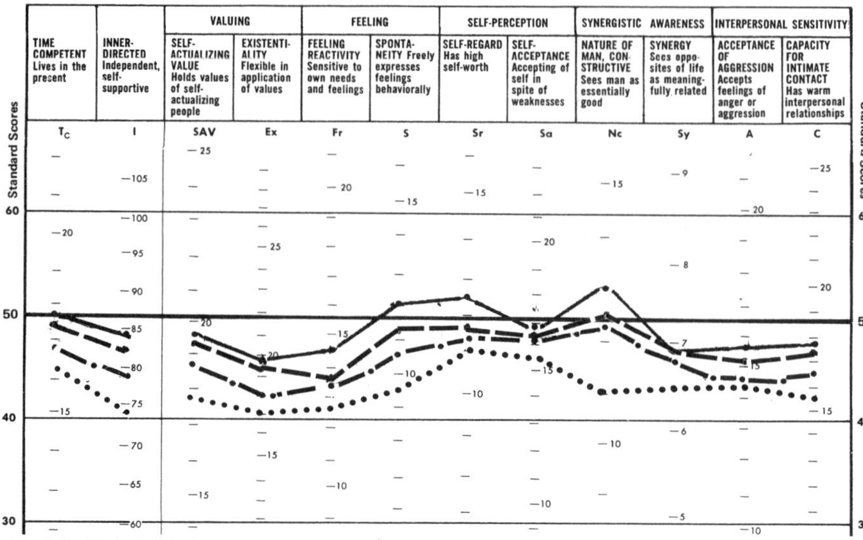

Age 26–35 (—) (N=218)
m 17.7 84.9 19.6 19.9 14.5 12.0 12.3 16.6 13.0 6.9 15.5 17.8
Age 36–45 (- - -) (N=300)
m 17.5 83.4 19.3 19.6 13.7 11.2 11.8 16.8 12.6 6.9 15.1 17.4
Age 46–55 (·—·—) (N=211)
m 16.9 79.3 18.7 18.0 13.2 10.4 11.6 16.4 12.3 6.8 14.8 16.3
Age 56+ (· · ·) (N=188)
m 16.4 74.7 17.8 17.0 12.4 9.3 11.0 15.3 11.0 6.5 14.1 15.6

Based on data reported by Greely (1970)

Figure 33. Age-Related Trends for POI Scores Among Catholic Priest Samples.

magnitude. Inner-Directed means for the four intervals considered were 74.3, 75.2, 76.6, and 76.9, which were not significantly different from one another. Rizzo and Vinacke (1973) also found a trend toward greater actualizing when comparing the college, mature adult and old samples in their study.

In conclusion, the trend of increasing actualization up to the early or middle adult years seems fairly well established. As yet the overall trend beyond ages thirty to forty is less clear-cut and more research is needed to clarify the interaction of age and actualizing tendencies with, perhaps, other moderating variables.

INTERRELATIONSHIPS AMONG THE SCALES

The concepts measured by the POI were not conceived as being independent or orthogonal. In fact, the subscales contain varying numbers of overlapping items. Thus, it is not surprising that most of the intercorrelations among subscales are positive, ranging in magnitude from .02 up to .64 between Feeling Reactivity and Acceptance of Aggression—this in a college sample of 138 reported by Knapp (1965) and shown in Table 7.

Table 7

Intercorrelational Matrix[1] for Personal Orientation Inventory

POI Scales		2	3	4	5	6	7	8	9	10	11	12
1. Time Competent	TC	.49	.26	.31	.20	.38	.44	.43	.19	.29	.17	.25
2. Inner-Directed	I		.54	.70	.58	.71	.62	.63	.37	.41	.61	.55
3. Self-Actualizing Value	SAV			.21	.23	.45	.56	.03	.41	.58	.32	.15
4. Existentiality	Ex				.32	.42	.32	.57	.27	.36	.39	.48
5. Feeling Reactivity	Fr					.44	.25	.21	-.03	.12	.64	.53
6. Spontaneity	S						.44	.40	.17	.30	.47	.30
7. Self-Regard	Sr							.21	.32	.26	.28	.23
8. Self-Acceptance	Sa								.24	.22	.32	.30
9. Nature of Man	Nc									.53	-.04	-.02
10. Synergy	Sy										.28	.14
11. Acceptance of Aggression	A											.44
12. Capacity for Intimate Contact	C											

[1]Correlations are based on a college sample of 128 from a report by Knapp (1965).

In commenting on item overlap that may in part account for the high correlation between Feeling Reactivity and Acceptance of Aggression, Bloxom (1972) notes that "both imply an awareness and acceptance of hostile feelings. Therefore it is not surprising that the scales for these two variables should have a number of items in common" (p. 291). Even in this case, each score accounts for less than half the variance of the other, allowing for considerable unique contribution to be made by each scale.

In comparing the degree of POI scale interrelatedness with the major factor-analytically derived instruments, the following comparative data are of interest. In the case of the POI, the median correlation based on the college sample is 130, excluding correlations against the Inner-Directed scale, which is the major overall estimate of actualizing. For the 16PF, which is admittedly based on an oblique-factor solution, intercorrelations range in magnitude from 0 to .75, with a median of approximately .14 (from Cattell, Eber, & Tatsuoka, 1970, p. 113). For the *Comrey Personality Scales*, intercorrelations range in magnitude from .01 to .47, with a median of .15 (from Comrey, 1970, p. 17), and for the *Guilford-Zimmerman Temperament Survey,* based on an orthogonal factor solution, intercorrelations range in magnitude from .01 to .69, with a median correlation of .235 (from Guilford & Zimmerman, 1949, p. 7). Only in Eysenck's two-, and now three-factor solution (Eysenck & Eysenck, 1975) do intercorrelations approach zero order.

Development of the POI was focused on maximizing convergent validity and interpretive usefulness rather than on homogeneity and factorial purity of the scales. Information such as that the POI subscale of Spontaneity is more effective in measuring pre- to post-test changes following encounter group experience (see Table 3, page 32), while the Time Competence and Synergy scales are more effective in differentiating normal from alcoholic samples (Zaccaria & Weir, 1967, p. 61) or normal from delinquent samples (see Figure 22, page 59, and Silverstein & Fisher, 1973), illustrates the kind of construct validity accumulating for POI scales.

Since the development of the POI some attention has been directed to the development of nonoverlapping scales for the POI. Silverstein and Fisher (1974) used a cluster analysis technique to define five cluster scales with nonoverlapping items. Aside from the reduced magnitude of intercorrelational coefficients and the somewhat increased internal consistency of the cluster scales, no evidence of their superiority was presented. As Silverstein and Fisher concluded, "A more basic question than the relationships between cluster scores and scale scores, and one that can only be answered by gathering additional empirical evidence, concerns their relative validity" (p. 329).

In a study by Knapp and Fitzgerald (1973), the validity of the published POI scale scores was compared with a set of nine "purified" research scales. The purpose of the study was to examine the comparative validity of the two sets of scales for predicting change following an encounter group experience. The "purified," nonoverlapping research scales were developed from a synthesis of analyses based on criterion-correlated and item factor analytic studies, the latter of which were those of Silverstein and Fisher (1974), Lorr and Knapp (1974), and Zimmerman. The POI was administered prior to a weekend marathon group experience and immediately following the workshop. Significant change scores (at the .01 confidence level) were obtained for five of the twelve published POI scales as compared with three of the nine research scales. The degree of separation between pre- and post-test scores appeared to be no greater for the research scales. Validity data for these purified research scales have been reported in only one other study, that of Lessner and Knapp (1974), and it is reported by the publisher of the POI that the demand for scoring for these purified scales has been less than overwhelming. In the present author's opinion and based on the evidence available to date it would appear that little is to be gained from attempts to restructure scoring of this particular instrument. The challenge of the many unique validating opportunities which yet exist is overwhelmingly intriguing!

FACTORIAL STUDIES

Several attempts have been made to study the POI in terms of factorial structure. Most of these attempts were confounded by methodological difficulties in submitting an instrument such as the POI to factor analysis. Early studies were based on scale intercorrelations, violating major principles of factor analysis and adding little to an understanding of the Inventory content or of the concept of self-actualizing.

Among the misuses of factor analysis summarized by Guilford (1952) and that are pertinent in reviewing such analysis of the POI are:

(a) the failure to isolate a common factor due to its being represented in only one experimental variable, thus ignoring Thurstone's (1947) admonition that at least three variables are necessary to determine a single common factor;
(b) the use of spurious correlations based on correlations between linearly dependent variables, such as scale scores in which the same items are scored for more than one trait variable;
(c) the use of correlations based on ipsative scores; and
(d) the use of heterogeneous samples.

To date, published factorial studies involving use of the POI generally may be divided into two categories: those employing scale scores and those considering results based upon item factor analyses. An example of the first category is the study by Tosi and Hoffman (1972), based on POI scale scores from 132 undergraduate college students. Scores from the ten subscales, as well as from the major scales of Time Competence and Inner-Directed (from which subscale items are derived) were included in the analysis. Tosi and Hoffman report three resulting factors that, on the basis of this analysis, they chose to interpret as "Extroversion, Open-Mindedness and Existential

Non-Conformity," elements certainly reflected in content of POI items. In concluding, the authors question the necessity of reporting results for as many scales as are incorporated in the POI and suggest reduction to three or four scales to facilitate interpretation. While, of course, the results of any factorial study employing scale scores would result in fewer second-order (super) factors (as in [a] above) such analyses are further complicated in the case of the POI by overlapping items ([b] above). To answer the methodological question "Is Item Overlap Responsible for a 'Built-In' Factor Structure?" Silverstein and Fisher (1968) factor analyzed POI scale scores from three samples. The resulting factor structure was compared to a factor analysis simply based on intercorrelations of the number of overlapping items on the POI scales. Similarity of the results was assessed by mean coefficients of congruence between the factors in the empirical data and those in the item overlap correlations. Coefficients of .91 for Factor I and .92 for Factor II led to the suggestion that item overlap may be responsible for the appearance of at least the first two of the three factors found in the empirical data. This study was repeated (Silverstein & Fisher, 1972) with much the same empirical findings and conclusions.

Le May and Damm (1970) administered the POI and the *Edwards Personal Preference Survey* (EPPS) to male and female college samples and submitted the intercorrelational matrices to factor analysis. Several instrument characteristics also probably confounded these results. The EPPS is a forced-choice (ipsative) instrument ([c] above) while the POI is a normative instrument, which complicates the intercorrelational process. Correlations in fact between the two instruments ranged from .00 to maximum magnitudes of only .34 and -.40 in the male and female samples respectively. Further, as in the Silverstein and Fisher (1968) analysis, the inclusion of a single estimate only for each POI scale could be expected to result only in second-order factors (or superfactors) numbering less than the original number of POI scales. The obtained factor structure was similar to that obtained by Silverstein and Fisher (1968). As in the earlier study, most of the POI scales loaded on the first factor, which was heavily loaded by the major POI scale I and the subscales Fr, S, A, and C. All subscale items in the POI, of course, contribute to the major I scale scores, thus confounding these results.

An alternative approach followed in attempting to arrive at a factorial solution to the content of the POI is to factor item responses. Such analyses, of course, result in scales of comparatively high homogeneity as well as being subject to inconsistencies resulting from the unreliability of single-item responses and to difficulty in obtaining otherwise homogeneous samples, which at the same time are differentiated by POI items at both extremes of degree of self-actualizing. However, in the case of the POI, such analyses might represent a first step in isolating dimensions of self-actualizing as represented in the POI. Silverstein and Fisher (1974) applied cluster analysis to POI responses from 500 male prisoners ranging in age from eighteen to sixty-seven. The analysis resulted in five major clusters that were interpretable in terms of corresponding POI scales. The five clusters were described by the authors as (I) Self-Acceptance; (II) Existentiality, A; (III) Nature of Man; (IV) Existentiality, C; and, (V) Spontaneity.

A subsequent item factor analytic study was that by Lorr and Knapp (1974), based on a comparatively more representative sample of 300, including professional persons, college students, and representatives of various professional occupational groups. Fifteen principal component factors were retained on the basis of Cattell's (1966) scree test and were rotated by varimax. Ten factors were interpretable:

(1) Self-Esteem (approximately matching Silverstein and Fisher's cluster I, Self-Acceptance);
(2) Adherence to Principles: Flexible versus Rigid (cutting across Silverstein and Fisher's clusters II and IV, Existentiality A and C);
(3) Freedom of Self-Expression;
(4) Sense of Obligation;
(5) Positive View of Human Nature;
(6) Self-Actualizing;
(7) Flexible versus Perfectionistic;
(8) Self-Accepting (overlapping in content with Silverstein and Fisher's cluster V, Spontaneity);
(9) Acceptance of Differences; and
(10) Acceptance of Aggression.

A major conclusion of this study was that "the POI reflects a fairly complex aggregation of factors."

In an extension of this study, Lorr (1973) submitted the responses from two other samples to the same factor analytic procedures. One of these samples consisted of college students and the other sample consisted of adult volunteers secured through a posted community request for such volunteers (Ommanny & Fifield, 1973). Attempts to match factors from sample to sample are far from satisfactory, with only about four of ten interpretable factors obtained in each analysis having a corresponding factor of similar content in each of the three analyses.

The error of claiming too many interpretable factors on the basis of item factor analysis is as misleading as claiming too few factors on the basis of scale intercorrelations, as in the Tosi and Hoffman (1972) study. Wright and Wyant (1974) submitted the responses of 393 students to the twenty-six items comprising the POI SAV scale to factor analysis and obtained nine factors, all of which were interpreted, even though six of the nine factors apparently were doublets, having only two defining items.

As previously noted, the POI was not designed for factor analytic approaches and does not lend itself to this technique. In line with Campbell and Fiske's (1959) "mono-trait-multi-method" principle, POI items reflecting each scale concept might be expected to display low homogeneity—that is, in general display low item intercorrelations reflecting broad, complex concepts rather than "narrow homogeneous" scales. In spite of this, scale reliability is in line with that of other personality scales and respectable estimates of homogeneity of scale, for example, have been reported.

Internal consistency coefficients of .75 for the Inner-Directed scale and .50 for the Time Competence scale have been reported by Silverstein and Fisher (1973). Similarly, Kaats (1973) has reported internal consistency coefficients of .80 for the Inner-Directed scale and .65 for the Time Competence scale. It is held that exploration with the POI of the humanistic concepts of self-actualizing is on firmer ground than would be the case of scale "dependence purely on the rickety foundation of single items." (See Cattell, 1972, p. 180; and Tsujioka & Cattell, 1964.)

The real test, of course, of the effectiveness of attempts to refine or alter scoring categories for the POI is whether such efforts result in increased validity. Very little evidence is available to date bearing on this issue. Knapp and Fitzgerald (1973) compared the validity of the published, theoretically developed POI scales with that of a set of nine research scales based on the series of item factor analyses conducted by Lorr, Silverstein, and Fisher and by Zimmerman, as described above. Although differing in item composition, the research scales are generally parallel in content to the logical scales and were identified by the interpretive title corresponding to the original scales. The criterion in this study was pre- to post-test gains in self-actualizing following a transgenerational (encounter) workshop experience. Five of the POI logical scales significantly increased (at the .01 level) following the workshop experience. These included the overall Inner-Directed scale as well as subscales of Feeling Reactivity (Fr), Spontaneity (S), Self-Regard (Sr), and Acceptance of Aggression (A). Among the POI research scales, three reached significance at the .01 level: Self-Regard (Sr_2), Acceptance of Aggression (A_2) and Capacity for Intimate Contact (C_2). As might be expected, overall differentiation would not be greatly different under the two scoring systems since scores, after all, are derived from the same pool of items. Examination of the comparative validity did not result in preference of the new scoring system over the original, as previously described in the section on Interrelationship Among the Scales.

SUMMARY

As evidenced by the wide variety of topics considered in the studies summarized in this volume, concepts measured by the POI have stimulated research into a broad spectrum of values and behavior seen to be important in the development of the actualizing person. The availability of a quantitative measure of such concepts has contributed greatly to the clarification and testing of theoretical hypotheses in this field of human behavior.

Major considerations contributing to the wide applicability of the POI certainly have been the objectivity of measurement, the positive, nonthreatening nature of the concepts measured, its resistance to faking, and the relevent "in the now" statement of items and description of the constructs. As Maslow (1971) noted about the POI, "It correlates well with external variables of various kinds and keeps on accumulating additional correlational meanings. As a result, I feel heuristically justified in *starting* with my 'determined naïveté.' Most of what I was able to see intuitively, directly, personally, is being confirmed now with numbers and tables and curves" (p. 28).

A number of studies based on diverse populations from widely disparate regions have demonstrated the validity of the POI as a measure of concepts considered to reflect "actualizing." For example, Shostrom's (1964) presentation of highly significant differences between clinically nominated actualizing and nonactualizing samples; Fox, Knapp, and Michael's (1968) demonstration of significantly lower scores for a hospitalized psychiatric population, and McClain's (1970b) quite substantial correlations between POI scores and supervisors' ratings of levels of actualizing among counselors provide strong evidence for the relevance of POI scores to behavioral indices judged to be important in development of the actualizing person.

Also of major importance are the number of studies showing the sensitivity of POI measures to changes resulting from various treatments. The demonstration by Shostrom and Knapp (1966) that advanced therapy patients score significantly higher on POI scales than beginning therapy patients is of moment. More impressive perhaps are the substantial number of studies, including the most recent research of Foulds and Hannigan (1976) and Nidich, Seeman, and Dreskin (1973), which demonstrate the sensitivity of the POI to changes resulting from group therapy techniques.

Of major interest in the design of future studies will be the differential predictive usefulness of the many concepts developed by Shostrom as well as the differential usefulness of these concepts in predicting diverse outside criteria.

DIRECTIONS FOR RESEARCH

Although a very impressive body of data now exists concerning research use of the POI, certain avenues of study stand out as areas particularly in need of consideration at this time. Only a few directions for research are suggested below and, clearly, investigators familiar with specific areas will propose more powerful and unique studies as research on concepts of the actualizing person progresses.

Effects of Treatment

The POI has been shown to be highly sensitive to the treatment effects of individual and group therapy. As a result of carefully controlled studies, such as that of Foulds and Hannigan (1976), the evidence in this regard is quite convincing. What is needed now are studies designed to assess the relative effectiveness of various treatment approaches and the interaction between personality styles of clients or participants and the counselor, therapist, or group leader.

Designs such as that suggested in Hood's (1968) research matching counselors identified as high or low actualizing with counselees identified according to levels of actualizing should be explored further. Effects of group therapy employing encounter techniques could be compared with those employing more nondirective techniques or other approaches.

Scale Validity and Profile Pattern Analysis

A great many of the validity studies summarized in this volume have been concerned with the relationship of levels of actualizing to various outside criteria. In many instances the POI has been used as an index of standing on an overall concept of actualizing. More research needs to be undertaken to determine the relative predictive usefulness of the many constructs underlying the overal concept of actualizing.

That time orientation is of major importance in consideration of the alcoholic, while changes in spontaneity are the most marked result of the group encounter experience, are very useful pieces of information in the interpretation of POI results. Such relationships can be extended through replication of result patterns in a wide variety of settings, as was the case with the group encounter results, and by carefully designed studies to determine patterns of relationships between subscales and specific criteria.

Relationship to Occupational Effectiveness

Studies such as those of McClain (1970) and Jansen, Bonk, and Garvey (in press) relating level of actualizing to ratings of success as counselors could be extended to other occupations. Also the effect of the level of actualizing on various criteria of outcome should be explored. Such studies could be extended to relationships between teachers and students, therapists and clients, and supervisors and subordinants.

Institutional Supportiveness

Assuming that personal actualizing is a goal affecting institutional policy, other studies should be undertaken to determine the effect of various policies on levels of actualizing of institutional members. The relationships presented by Greeley (1970) between encyclicals of the Catholic Church and levels of actualizing of priests are examples of evidence that might be used in weighing effects of institutional policy. Results of application of this method in educational and industrial organizations are to be looked forward to.

Educational Application

A few studies have been concerned with the relationship of levels of actualizing to academic success. The interesting finding by Le May (1969) of a moderator effect in which relationships between actualizing and grade point average are greatest among middle ability students should be replicated and clarified. Also, results relating teacher level of actualizing to teacher effectiveness could be extended to cover other, particularly noncognitive, subjects. Weinrach's (1972) finding that levels of counselor actualizing are related to students' ratings of the effectiveness of the guidance program should be extended. Finally, studies should be designed to determine which students respond best to different instructional approaches as well as the most effective matching of teacher and student characteristics.

BIBLIOGRAPHY

PRIMARY REFERENCES: PUBLISHED ARTICLES

Abbott, R.D., & Harris, L. Social desirability and phychometric characteristics of the Personal Orientation Inventory. *Educational and Psychological Measurement*, 1973, 33, 427-432.

Alperson, B.L., Alperson, E., & Levine, R. Growth effects of high school marathons. Experimental Publications System, Feb. 1971, 10, Ms. No. 369-56.

Archer, J., & Kagan, N. Teaching interpersonal relationship skills on campus: a pyramid approach. *Journal of Counseling Psychology*, 1973, 20, 535-540.

Banmen, J., & Capelle, R. Human-relations training in three rural Manitoba high schools: a three-month follow up. *Canadian Counsellor*, 1972, 6, 260-270

Bebout, J. & Gordon, B. The value of encounter. In L.N. Solomon & Betty Berzon (Eds.) *New Perspectives on Encounter Groups*. San Francisco: Jossey-Bass, 1972.

Bloxom, B. Review of the Personal Orientation Inventory. In O.K. Buros (Ed.), *The Seventh Mental Measurements Yearbook*. Highland Park, N.J.: Gryphon Press, 1972. 290-292.

Braun, J.R. Effects of "typical neurotic" and "after therapy" sets on Personal Orientation Inventory scores. *Psychological Reports*, 1966, 19, 1282.

Braun, J.R. Search for correlates of self-actualization. *Perceptual and Motor Skills*, 1969, 28, 557-558.

Braun, J.R., & Asta, P. Intercorrelations between Personal Orientation Inventory and Gordon Personal Inventory scores. *Psychological Reports*, 1968, 23, 1197-1198.

Braun, J.R., & Asta, P. A comparison of "real" versus "ideal" self with a self-actualization inventory. *The Journal of Psychology*, 1969, 72, 159-164.

Braun, J.R., & La Faro, D. A further study of the fakability of the Personal Orientation Inventory. *Journal of Clinical Psychology*, 1969, 25, 296-299.
Brockopp, G.W., & Lester, D. Time competence and suicidal history. *Psychological Reports*, 1971, 28, 80.
Byrd, R.E. Training in a non-group. *Journal of Humanistic Psychology*, 1967, 18-27.
Coan, R.W. Review of the Personal Orientation Inventory, In O.K. Buros (Ed.), *The Seventh Mental Measurements Yearbook*. Highland Park, N.J.: Gryphon Press, 1972, 292-294.
Coble, C.R. Self-actualization and the effective biology teacher. *The American Biology Teacher*, 1973, 35, 479-481.
Coble, C.R., & Hounshell, P.B. Teacher self-actualization and student progress, *Science Education*, 1972, 56, 311-316.
Collins, B.E., Martin, J.C., Ashmore, R.D., & Ross, L. Some dimensions of the internal-external metaphor in theories of personality. *Journal of Personality*, in press.
Constantine, L.L., & Constantine, J.M. *The group marriage experiments: a study of contemporary multilateral marriage.* New York: Macmillan, 1973.
Cooper, C.L. T-group training and self-actualization. *Psychological Reports*, 1971, 28, 391-394.
Crosson, S. & Schwendiman, G. Self-actualization as a predictor of conformity behavior. Unpublished manuscript, Marshall University, 1972.
Counseling Center Staff, University of Massachusetts. Effects of three types of sensitivity groups on changes in measures of self-actualization. *Journal of Counseling Psychology*, 1972, 19, 253-254.
Cryns, A.G. Personality characteristics of heroin addicts in a methadone treatment program: An exploratory study. *The International Journal of the Addictions*, 1974, 9, 255-266.
Culbert, S.A., Clark, J.V., & Bobele, H.K. Measures of change toward self-actualization in two sensitivity training groups. *Journal of Counseling Psychology*, 1968, 15, 53-57.
Damm, V.J. Overall measures of self-actualization derived from the Personal Orientation Inventory. *Educational and Psychological Measurement*, 1969, 29, 977-981.
Damm, V.J. Creativity and intelligence: Research implications for equal emphasis in high school. *Exceptional Children*, 1970, 36, 565-569.
Damm, V.J. Overall measures of self-actualization derived from the Personal Orientation Inventory: A replication and refinement study. *Educational and Psychological Measurement*, 1972, 32, 485-489.
Dandes, H.M. Psychological health and teaching effectiveness. *Journal of Teacher Education*, 1966, 17, 301-306.
Doyle, J.A. Field-independence and self-actualization. *Psychological Reports*, 1975, 36, 363-366. (a)
Doyle, J..A. Self-actualization and attitudes toward women. *Psychological Reports,* 1975, 37, 899-902. (b)

Emrick, C.D. Abstinence and time perception of alcoholics. *Quarterly Journal of Studies in Alcoholism*, 1970, 31, 384-393.

Fisher, G. Performance of psychopathic felons on a measure of self-actualization. *Educational and Psychological Measurement*, 1968, 28, 561-563.

Fisher, G. Self-actualization of "paranormals." *Journal of Personality Assessment*, 1971, 35, 486-491.

Fisher, G. Felons' conception of societal self-actualization values. *Corrective Psychiatry*, 1973, 19, 3-5.

Fisher, G., & Silverstein, A.B. Simulation of poor adjustment on a measure of self-actualization. *Journal of Clinical Psychology*, 1969, 25, 198-199. (a)

Fisher, G., & Silverstein, A.B. Self-actualization values of felons. *Journal of Humanistic Psychology*, 1969, 9, 66-70. (b)

Foulds, M.L. Positive mental health and facilitative genuineness during counseling. *Personnel and Guidance Journal*, 1969, 47, 762-766. (a)

Foulds, M.L. Self-actualization and level of counselor interpersonal functioning. *Journal of Humanistic Psychology*, 1969, 9, 87-92. (b)

Foulds, M.L. Self-actualization and the communication of facilitative conditions during counseling. *Journal of Counseling Psychology*, 1969, 16, 132-136. (c)

Foulds, M.L. Effects of a personal growth group on a measure of self-actualization. *Journal of Humanistic Psychology*, 1970, 10, 33-38.

Foulds, M.L. Measured changes in self-actualization as a result of a growth group experience. *Psychotherapy: Theory, Research and Practice*, 1971, 8, 338-341.

Foulds, M.L., Guinan, J.F., & Hannigan, P.S. The marathon group: Changes in a measure of self-actualization, in press.

Foulds, M.L., & Hannigan, P.S. Gestalt marathon workshops: A further test of the self-actualization hypothesis. Manuscript submitted for publication, 1975. (c)

Foulds, M.L., & Hannigan, P.S. Effects of gestalt marathon groups on measured self-actualization: A replication and follow-up study. *Journal of Counseling Psychology*, 1976, 23, 60-65.

Foulds, M.L., & Hannigan, P.S. Gestalt marathon group: Does it increase reported self-actualization? *Psychotherapy: Theory, Research and Practice*, in press.

Foulds, M.L., & Warehime, R.G. Effects of a "fake good" response set on a measure of self-actualization. *Journal of Counseling Psychology*, 1971, 18, 279-280. (a)

Foulds, M.L., & Warehine, R.G. Relationship between repression-sensitization and a measure of self-actualization. *Journal of Consulting and Clinical Psychology*, 1971, 36, 257-259. (b)

Foulds, M.L., Wright, J.C., & Guinan, J.F. Marathon group: a six-month follow-up. *Journal of College Student Personnel*, 1970, 11, 426-431.

Fox, J., Knapp, R.R., & Michael W.B. Assessment of self-actualization of psychiatric patients: Validity of the Personal Orientation Inventory. *Educational and Psychological Measurement*, 1968, 28, 565-569.

Freeman, H.R., & Brubaker, P. Personality characteristics of campus demonstrators compared to nondemonstrators. *Journal of Counseling Psychology*, 1971, 18, 462-464.

Gelfand, B. Self-actualization tendencies of children's aid society workers. Toronto, Ontario, Canada: Ministry of Community and Social Services, Training Report 11, 1974.

Gibb, L.L. Home background and self-actualization attainment. *Journal of College Student Personnel*, 1968, 49-53.

Gilligan, J.F. Personality characteristics of selectors and nonselectors of sensitivity training. *Journal of Counseling Psychology*, 1973, 20, 265-268.

Graff, R.W., & Bradshaw, H.E. Relationship of a measure of self-actualization to dormitory assistant effectiveness. *Journal of Counseling Psychology*, 1970, 17, 502-505.

Graff, R.W., Bradshaw, H.E., Danish, S.J., Austin, B.A., & Altekruse, M. The POI: A validity check. *Educational and Psychological Measurement*, 1970, 30, 429-432.

Graff, R.W., & Ladd, C.E. POI correlates of a religious commitment inventory. *Journal of Clinical Psychology*, 1971, 27, 502-504.

Grossack, M.M., Armstrong, T., & Lussiev, G. Correlates of self-actualization. *Journal of Humanistic Psychology*, 1966, 6, 87-88.

Guinan, J.F., & Foulds, M.L. Marathon group: Facilitator of personal growth? *Journalof Counseling Psychology*, 1970, 17, 145-149.

Gunter, L.M. The developing nursing student: Part 1, A study of self-actualizing values. *Nursing Research*, 1969, 18, 60-64.

Hamilton, J.T. Educational administrators and their level of self-actualization. *Education Leadership*, 1971, 28, 633-635.

Harvey, V., DiLuzio, G., & Hunter, W.J. Effects of verbal and non-verbal T-groups on personality and attitudinal variables. *Journal of Applied Behavioral Science*, in press.

Hekmat, H., & Theiss, M. Self-actualization and modification of affective self-disclosures during a social conditioning interview. *Journal of Counseling Psychology*, 1971, 18, 101-105.

Hjelle, L.A., & Butterfield, R. Self-actualization and women's attitudes toward their roles in contemporary society. *The Journal of Psychology*, 1974, 87, 225-230.

Ilardi, R.L., & May, W.T. A reliability study of Shostrom's Personal Orientation Inventory. *Journal of Humanistic Psychology*, 1968, 68-72.

Insko, W.R. Developing family actualization: The Frankfort project. *Family Coordinator*, 1971, 20, 17-22.

Jansen, D.G. Personal communication, 1974.

Jansen, D.G., Garvey, F.J., & Bonk, E.C. Personality characteristics of clergyman entering a clinical training program at a state hospital. *Psychological Reports*, 1972, 31, 878.

Jansen, D.G., & Garvey, F.J. High-average- and low-rated clergymen in a state hospital clinical program. *Journal of Clinical Psychology*, 1973, 29, 89-92.

Jansen, D.G., Bonk, E.C., & Garvey, F.J. Relationships between Personal Orientation Inventory and Shipley-Hartford scale scores and supervisor and peer ratings of counseling competency for clergymen in clinical training. *Journal of Community Psychology*, in press.

Jansen, D.G., & Garvey, F.J. Self-actualization of high- and low-rated clergymen in a state hospital clinical and counseling training program, *Counselor Education and Supervision,* in press.

Jansen, D.G., Garvey, F.J., & Bonk, E.C. Another look at intercorrelations among scales of Personal Orientation Inventory, *Psychological Reports*, in press.

Jansen, D.G., Knapp, R.R., & Knapp, L. Measurement of personality change in an alcoholic treatment program: Further validation of the Personal Orientation Dimensions. *Educational and Psychological Measurement*, 1976, in press.

Johns, D.J. Correlations of *Personal Orientation Inventory* scores with first quarter freshmen grade point averages. *Student Affairs Research Newsletter, Washington Technical Institute*, 1970, 1, 1-4.

Kaats, BA. Personal communication, 1973.

Kammeier, M.L. Adolescents from families with and without alcohol problems. *Quarterly Journal of Studies on Alcohol*, 1971, 32, 364-372.

Kennedy, E.C., & Heckler, V.J. The Loyola psychological study of the ministry and life of the American priest. National Conference of Catholic Bishops, 1971.

Kilmannn, P.R. Direct and nondirect marathon group therapy and internal-external control. *Journal of Counseling Psychology*, 1974, 21, 380-384.

Kilmann, P.R. Self-actualization of female narcotic drug addicts. *The Journal of Clinical Psychology*, 1974, 308-310.

Kilmann, P.R., & Howell, R.J. The effects of structure of marathon group therapy and locus of control on therapeutic outcome. *Journal of Consulting and Clinical Psychology*, 1974, 42, 912.

Kimball, R., & Gelso, C.J. Self-actualization in a marathon growth group: Do the strong get stronger? *Journal of Counseling Psychology*, 1974, 21, 38-42.

Klavetter, R.E., & Mogar, R.E. Stability and internal consistency of a measure of self-actualization. *Psychological Reports*, 1967, 21, 422-424.

Knapp, R.R. Relationship of a measure of self-actualization to neuroticism and extraversion. *Journal of Consulting Psychology*, 1965, 29, 168-172.

Knapp, R.R. *The measurement of self-actualization and its theoretical implications*. San Diego: Educational and Industrial Testing Service, 1971.

Knapp, R.R., & Comrey, A.L. Further construct validation of a measure of self-actualization. *Educational and Psychological Measurement*, 1973, 33, 419-425.

Knapp, R.R., & Fitzgerald, O.R. Comparative validity of the logically developed versus "purified" research scales for the Personal Orientation Inventory. *Educational and Psychological Measurement*, 1973, 33, 971-976.

Kramer, M., McDonnell, C., & Reed, J.L. Self-actualization and role adaptation of baccalaureate degree nurses. *Nursing Research*, 1972, 21, 111-123.

Lafferty, J.C. Personal communication, Februay 21, 1969.

Leib, J.W., & Snyder, W.U. Effects of group discussions on underachievement and self-actualization. *Journal of Counseling Psychology*, 1967, 14, 282-285.

Leib, J.W., & Snyder, W.U. Achievement and positive mental health: A supplementary report. *Journal of Counseling Psychology*, 1968, 15, 388-389.

LeMay, M.L. Self-actualization and college achievement at three ability levels. *Journal of Counseling Psychology*, 1969, 16, 582-583.

LeMay, M.L., & Damm, V.J. The Personal Orientation Inventory as a measure of the self-actualization of underachievers. *Measurement and Evaluation in Guidance*, 1968, 1, 110-114.

LeMay, M.L., & Damm, V.J. Relationship of the Personal Orientation Inventory to the Edwards Personal Preference Schedule. *Psychological Reports*, 1969, 24, 834.

LeMay, M.L., & Damm, V.J. Factor analysis of the Personal Orientation Inventory and Edwards Personal Preference Schedule. *Experimental Publication System*, 1970, 7, ms. no. 262-2.

Lessner, M., & Knapp, R.R. Self-actualization and entrepreneurial orientation among small business owners. A validation study of the POI. *Educational and Psychological Measurement*, 1974, 34, 455-460.

Lorr, M. Personal communication, 1973.

Lorr, M., & Knapp, R.R. Analysis of a self-actualization scale: The POI. *The Journal of Clinical Psychology*, 1974, 355-357.

Margulies, N. Organizational culture and psychological growth. *Applied Behavioral Science*, 1969, 5, 491-508.

Marks, S.E., Conry, R.F., & Foster, S.F. The marathon group hypothesis: An unanswered question. *Journal of Counseling Psychology*, 1973, 20, 185-187.

Mattocks, A.L., & Jew, C.C. Comparison of self-actualization levels and adjustment scores of incarcerated male felons. *Educational & Psychological Measurement*, 1974, 34, 69-74.

Mazer, G.E., & Engle, K.B. Personality and attitude change in counselor trainees: An evaluation. *Counsel Education and Supervision*, 1971, 10, 273-281.

McClain, E.W. Personal growth for teachers in training through self-study. *Journal of Teacher Education*, 1970, 21, 372-377. (a)

McClain, E.W. Further validation of the Personal Orientation Inventory: Assessment of self-actualization of school counselors. *Journal of Consulting and Clinical Psychology*, 1970, 35, 21-22. (b)

McClain, E.W., & Andrews, H.B. Self-actualization among extremely superior students. *Journal of College Student Personnel,* 1972, 505-510.

Meredith, G.M. Temperament and self-actualization. *EITS Research and Developments*, 1967, 1.

Morris, G.B. An empirical investigation: Rogers and Ellis. Manuscript submitted for publication, 1974.

Mullins, R.F., & Perkins, E.M. Increased self-actualization as a result of an intensive one-semester academic program. *Journal of Educational Research*, 1973, 66, 210-214.

Mullozzi, A., & Spees, E.R. Factors in selecting residence hall fellows. *Journal of the National Association of Women Deans and Counselors*, 1971, 34, 185-190.

Nidich, S., Seeman, W., & Dreskin, T. Influence of transcendental meditation: A replication. *Journal of Counseling Psychology*, 1973, 20, 565-566.

Noll, G.A., & Watkins, J.T. Differences between persons seeking encounter group experiences and others on the Personal Orientation Inventory. *Journal of Counseling Psychology*, 1974, 21, 206-209.

Osman, J.D. The use of selected value-clarifying strategies in health education. *The Journal of School Health*, 1974, 44, 21-25.

Pasnak, M.F.D., & Ayres, R.W. Clothing attitudes and personality characteristics of fashion innovators. *Journal of Home Economics*, 1969, 61, 689-702.

Phelan, J.G., Brooks, R., & Brashears, G.C. Relationship of kinesthetic figural aftereffect to masculinity-femininity and expectation for internal versus external control of reinforcement. *Perceptual and Motor Skills*, 1970, 31, 863-866.

Phillips, W.M., Watkins, J.T., & Noll, G. Self-actualization, self-transcendence, and personal philosophy. *Journal of Humanistic Psychology*, 1974, 14, 53-73.

Potkay, C.R. Simulated test-taking as a teaching technique: Freud, hemingway, and Jenny. *Journal of Humanistic Psychology*, 1973, 13, 69-73.

Potkay, C.R., Allen, B.P., & Haapoja, N. Use of the adjective generation technique in a therapy context: Case application. *Psychotherapy: Theory, Research and Practice*, 1973, 10, 343-347.

Raanan, S.L. Test review. *Journal of Counseling Psychology*, 1973, 20, 477-478.

Reddy, W.B. Interpersonal compatibility and self-actualization in sensitivity training. *Journal of Applied Behavioral Science*, 1972, 8, 237-240. (a)

Reddy, W.B. On affection, group composition, and self-actualization in sensitivity training. *Journal of Consulting and Clinical Psychology*, 1972, 38, 211-214. (b)

Reddy, W.B. The impact of sensitivity training on self-actualization: A one-year follow-up. *Small Group Behavior*, 1973, 4, 407-413.

Rizzo, R., & Vinacke, W.E. Self-actualization and the meaning of critical experience. *Journal of Humanistic Psychology*, 1975, 15, 19-29.

Rowe, W. The effect of "faking good" on the Personal Orientation Inventory. *Measurement and Evaluation in Guidance*. 1973, 6, 164-167.

Rowe, W., & Winborn, B.B. Self-actualization and counselor interpersonal functioning: A replication. *Journal of Humanistic Psychology*, 1973, 13, 79-84.

Rueveni, U., Swift, M., & Bell, A.A. II. Sensitivity training: Its impact on mental health workers. *Applied Behavioral Science*, 1969, 5, 600-601.

Sands, B.L. Relationship between family life teachers' self-actualization and self-perception of competency. *Journal of Home Economics*, 1971, 63, 113-115.

Savage, C., McCabe, O.L., Olsson, J.E., Unger, S., & Kurland, A.A. *Research with psychedelic drugs*. New York: Grune & Stratton, 1969.

Seeman, W., Nidich, S., & Banta, T. Influence of transcendental meditation on a measure of self-actualization. *Journal of Counseling Psychology*, 1972, 19, 184-187.

Sheridan, K., & Shack, J.R. Personality correlates of the undergraduate volunteer subject. *The Journal of Psychology*, 1970, 76, 23-26.

Shostrom, E.L. *Personal Orientation Inventory*. San Diego, California: EdITS/Educational & Industrial Testing Service, 1963.

Shostrom, E.L. An inventory for the measurement of self-actualization. *Educational and Psychological Measurement*, 1964, 24, 207-218.

Shostrom, E.L. Time as an integrating factor, In Buhler, C., & Massarik, (Eds.) *The course of human life: A study of goals in the humanistic perspective*. New York: Springer, 1968, 351-359.

Shostrom, E.L. *Manual for the Personal Orientation Inventory*. San Diego, Calif.: EdITS/Educational and Industrial Testing Service, 1974.

Shostrom, E.L. The measurement of growth in psychotherapy. *Psychotherapy: Theory, Research and Practice*, 1972, 9, 194-198.

Shostrom, E.L. Comment on a test review: The Personal Orientation Inventory. *Journal of Counseling Psychology*, 1973, 20, 479-481. (a)

Shostrom, E.L. From abnormality to actualization. *Psychotherapy: Theory, Research and Practice*. 1973, 10, 36-40. (b)

Shostrom, E.L. Self-actualization: A scientific ethic. *The Counseling Psychologist*, 1973, 4, 29-35. (c)

Shostrom, E.L., & Knapp, R.R. The relationship of a measure of self-actualization (POI) to a measure of pathology (MMPI) and to therapeutic growth. *American Journal of Psychotherapy*, 1966, 20, 193-202.

Shostrom, E.L., Knapp, L.F., & Knapp, R.R. *Actualizing Therapy: Foundations for a Scientific Ethic*. San Diego: EdITS, 1976.

Shostrom, E.L., Knapp, R.R., & Knapp, L. Validation of the Personal Orientation Dimensions. An inventory for the measurement of dimensions of actualizing. *Educational and Psychological Measurement*, 1976, in press.

Silverstein, A.B., & Fisher, G. Is item overlap responsible for a "built-in" factor structure? *Psychological Reports*, 1968, 23, 935-938.

Silverstein, A.B., & Fisher, G. Item overlap and the "built-in" factor structure of the Personal Orientation Inventory. *Psychological Reports*, 1972, 31, 492-494. (a)

Silverstein, A.B., & Fisher, G. Scale membership and direction of scoring for items on the Personal Orientation Inventory. *Psychological Reports*, 1972, 31, 663-665. (b)

Silverstein, A.B., & Fisher, G. Internal consistency of POI scales. *Psychological Reports*, 1973, 32, 33-34.

Silverstein, A.B., & Fisher, G. Cluster analysis of Personal Orientation Inventory items in a prison sample. *Multivariate Behavioral Research*, 1974, 9, 325-330.

Smith, D.L. Goal attainment scaling as an adjunct to counseling. *Journal of Counseling Psychology*, 1976, 23, 22-27.

Smith, R. Repression-sensitization related to a measure of self-actualization. *Proceedings of the West Virginia Academy of Sciences*, 1971, 42, 262-266.

Stewart, R.A.C. Academic performance and components of self-actualization. *Perceptual and Motor Skills*, 1968, 26, 918.

Stewart, R.A.C., & Webster, A.C. Scale for theological conservatism, and its personality correlates. *Perceptual and Motor Skills*, 1970, 30, 867-870.

Tapp, J.T., & Spanier, D. Personal Characteristics of volunteer phone counselors. *Journal of Consulting and Clinical Psychology*, 1973, 41, 245-250.

Tosi, D.J., & Hoffman, S. A factor analysis of the Personal Orientation Inventory. *Journal of Humanistic Psychology*, 1972, 12, 86-93.

Travis, P.Y., & Travis, R.P. Self-actualization in marital enrichment. Manuscript submitted for publication, 1975. (a)

Travis, R.P., & Travis, P.Y. The pairing enrichment program: Actualizing the marriage. *The Family Coordinator*, 1975, 24, 161-165. (b)

Travis, R.P., & Travis, P.Y. Marital health and marriage enrichment. *Alabama Journal of Medical Sciences*, 12, 1975. (c)

Treppa, J.A., & Fricke, L. Effects of a marathon group experience. *Journal of Counseling Psychology*, 1972, 19, 466-467.

Trotter, A.B., Uhlig, G.E., & Fargo, G.E. Self-actualization as a predictor of rehabilitation counselor success. *Rehabilitation Counseling Bulletin*, 1971, 15, 58-67.

Uhes, M.J., & Shybut, J. Personal Orientation Inventory as a predictor of success in Peace Corps training. *Journal of Applied Psychology*, 1971, 55, 498-499.

Uhlig, G.E., Trotter, A.B., Gozali, J., & Tesch, M.J. Self-actualization in hospitalized disabled and non-hospitalized adults as measured by the Personal Orientation Inventory. *Psychological Aspects of Disability*, 1970, 17, 83-85.

VanderWilt, R.B. Self-actualization of females in an experimental orientation program. *Journal of the National Association of Women Deans and Counselors*, 1971, Spring, 125-129.

Wall, J.B. Relationships of locus of control to self-actualization. *Psychological Reports*, 1970, 27, 282.

Walton, D.R. Effects of personal growth groups on self-actualization and creative personality. *Journal of College Student Personnel*, 1973, 490-494.

Warehime, R.G., & Foulds, M.L. Perceived locus of control and personal adjustment. *Journal of Consulting and Clinical Psychology*, 1971, 37, 250-252.

Warehime, R.G., & Foulds, M.L. Social desirability response sets and a measure of self-actualization. *Journal of Humanistic Psychology*, 1973, 13, 89-95.

Warehime, R.G., Routh, D.K., & Foulds, M.L. Knowledge about self-actualization and the presentation of self as self-actualized. *Journal of Personality and Social Psychology*, 1974, 30, 155-162.

Webster, A.C. Factor analysis of family attitudes, cooperation, personality, and personal orientation in a small New Zealand sample. *Personality*, 1971, 2, 249-266.

Webster, A.C., & stewart, R.A.C. Psychological attitudes and beliefs of ministers. *Anvil Quarterly*, 1969, 1, 11-16.

Weinrach, S.G. Level of school counselor actualizing and student perception of guidance services: Further validation of the Personal Orientation Inventory. *Educational and Psychological Measurement*, 1976, in press.

Weir, W.R., & Gade, E.M. An approach to counseling alcoholics. *Rehabilitation Counseling Bulletin*, 1969, 12, 227-230.

White, J. The human potential laboratory in the community college. *Journal of College Student Personnel*, 1974, 15, 96-100.

Wills, B.S Personality variables which discriminate between groups differing in level of self-actualization. *Journal of Counseling Psychology*, 1974, 21, 222-227.

Winborn, B.B., & Rowe, W. Self-actualization and the communication of facilitative conditions—A replication. *Journal of Counseling Psychology*, 1972, 19, 26-29.

Wise, G.W., & Davis, J.E. The Personal Orientation Inventory: Internal consistency, stability, and sex differences. *Psychological Reports*, 1975, 36, 847-855.

Wright, L., & Wyant, K. Factor structure of self-actualization as measured from Shostrom's SAV scale. Unpublished manuscript, 1974.

Young, E.R., & Jacobson, L.I. Effects of time-extended marathon group experiences on personality characteristics. *Journal of Counseling Psychology*, 1970, 17, 247-251.

Zaccaria, J.S., & Weir, W.R. A comparison of alcoholics and selected samples of nonalcoholics in terms of a positive concept of mental health. *Journal of Social Psychology*, 1967, 71, 151-157.

Zimmerman, S.F., Pedersen, D.M., & Smith, K.H. The factorial determination of types of conforming individuals. *Journal of Psychology*, 1969, 72, 101-107.

Zimmerman, S.F., Smith, K.H., & Pedersen, D.M. The effect of anticonformity appeals on conformity behavior. *The Journal of Social Psychology*, 1970, 81, 93-103.

PRIMARY REFERENCES: DISSERTATIONS, PAPERS, AND UNPUBLISHED ARTICLES

Acker, M.B. The relationship of achievement, need, time perspective, and field articulation to academic performance. Unpublished doctoral dissertation, University of California at Berkeley, 1967.

Adams, N.G. A comparison between scores on a measure of self-actualization and peer group evaluations: A validity study of the POI for chaplains and trainees in mental health professions. Unpublished masters thesis, George Washington University, 1974.

Aikins, T.R. The effects of a marathon group experience on the attitudes and counseling effectiveness of counselor trainees. Unpublished masters thesis, University of Utah, 1971.

Alexander, J. A correlation between self-actualization and communications behavior. Unpublished masters thesis, University of the Pacific, 1971.

Anzalone, T. Personality characteristics relevant to research in human relations training. Unpublished doctoral dissertation, University of Nevada, 1971.

Aubry, W.E. An analysis of a one-week workshop for developing self-actualization and effective interpersonal behavior. Unpublished doctoral dissertation, The University of Arizona, 1970.

Ball, W.R. Physical contact as a variable in encounter group programming of counselors in training. Unpublished doctoral dissertation, Indiana University, 1971.

Banmen, J., & Capelle, R. Human relations training in three rural Manitoba high schools. Paper presented at the Convention of the National Council on Human Relations, Winnipeg, Canada, April 1971.

Barnett, L.C.F. The effect of silent communications upon counseling processes: An experimental study. The relevance of nonverbal behavior and self-actualization for counselor empathy and genuineness and client self-exploration. Unpublished doctoral dissertation, University of Missouri, 1971.

Bellanti, John. The effects of an encounter group experience on self-actualization and on three facilitative conditions of a counseling relation: Empathy, respect, and congruence. Unpublished dissertation, Penn State University, 1971.

Bertoch, M.R. A study of the relationship of counseling theory concepts to the self-concepts and values of counselors in training. Unpublished doctoral dissertation, Boston University, 1967.

Bishop, H.C. The relationship of organizational climate to psychological health of school administrators in selected black and white elementary schools of Florida. Unpublished doctoral dissertation, Syracuse University, 1971.

Blair, C.E. An examination of the relationship of the POI to rated success of superintendents. Unpublished doctoral dissertation, University of Indiana, 1970.

Boehme, L.C. Persuasibility and visual perception of a dress design as related to selected personality characteristics. Unpublished doctoral dissertation, Pennsylvania State University, 1970.

Bosbyshell, W.A. Some correlates of empathic behavior of Episcopal clergymen. Unpublished doctoral dissertation, University of Miami, 1970.

Boston, B.D. Self-actualization as a predictor of teaching success in individually guided education. Unpublished doctoral dissertation, Bowling Green State University, 1975.

Bouverat, R.A. A study of self-actualization and perceptions of teaching roles of prospective teachers of young children. Unpublished doctoral dissertation, Ohio State University, 1970.

Brenden, H.A. A study of the effects of induced anxiety and induced relaxation upon the performance of subjects on the Personal Orientation Inventory. Unpublished doctoral dissertation, Ball State University, 1970.

Brennan, L. The correlation of self-actualization, selected background variables, and involvement in social organizations and activities of women in three national Catholic organizations. Unpublished doctoral dissertation, Boston College, 1973.

Burdg, M. Relationship of student attrition rates and self-actualization of community college teachers. Unpublished doctoral dissertation, United States International University, 1970.

Burke, J. The relationship between religious orientation and self-actualization among selected Catholic groups. Unpublished doctoral dissertation, United States International University, 1973.

Burkhalter, P.K. Concern about leakage, gas and odor as factors influencing social contact, anxiety and self-acceptance of individuals with colostomy. Unpublished thesis, University of Hawaii, 1969.

Byrd, R.E. Training clergy for creative risk taking: A preliminary evaluation. Paper read at S.S.S.R. meetings, October 1966.

Byrd, R.E. Self-actualization through creative risk taking: A new laboratory model. *Dissertation Abstracts International,* Vol. XXXI, Number 12, 1971.

Cain, A.O. The relationship between growth in self-actualization and the numbers of perceived and mutually perceived relationships in sensitivity training groups. Unpublished doctoral dissertation, University of Maryland, 1972.

Carpenter, J.C. Patterns of self-disclosure and confirmation in mother-daughter communication. Unpublished doctoral dissertation, Ohio State University, 1970.

Chedekel, D.S. The levels of anxiety and self-actualization in dropout-prone ninth grade boys. Unpublished doctoral dissertation, Boston University, 1971.

Coble, C.R. An analysis of the relationship between the biology teacher's level of self-actualization and student progress. Unpublished doctoral dissertation, University of North Carolina, 1971.

Cohen, A.W. Some factors relating to the attrition of beginning teachers from inner-city schools: Predictors for improved recruitment. Unpublished doctoral dissertation, University of Connecticut, 1971.

Cohen, E.D. Some related variables in the interpersonal risk (IR) theory. Unpublished doctoral dissertation, Case Western Reserve University, 1968.

Dale, V.M. An exploration of the relationship of home managers' self-actualization to participation by family members in home activities. Unpublished doctoral dissertation, University of Massachusetts, 1968.

Damm, V.J. The relationship of ego-strength to creativity and intelligence in high school students. Unpublished doctoral dissertation, University of Oregon, 1967.

Davies, M.M. A comparison of the effects of sensitivity training and programmed instruction on the development of human relations skills of beginning nursing students. Unpublished doctoral dissertation, Saint Louis University, 1970.

Davis, J.B. An investigation of the utility of Sixteen Personality Factor Questionnaire scores in predicting counseling effectiveness. Unpublished doctoral dissertation, University of Southern Mississippi, 1971.

Dawson, F. An analytical study of the effects of maternal employment, of same-sex chum denial in preadolescence, and of residential mobility of self-actualization. Unpublished doctoral dissertation, American University, 1969.

Deiulio, R.S. An analysis of college freshmen perceptions of staff members who functioned as counselors compared to those who functioned as teachers and counselors. Unpublished doctoral dissertation, Boston University, 1970.

Delaney, E.T. The effects of a group experience on the self-awareness of supervisor trainees and teacher trainees in supervision. Unpublished doctoral dissertation, University of Illinois, 1970.

De Loach, C.P. Effects of a group experience on the effectiveness of teaching assistants. Unpublished doctoral dissertation, University of Illinois, 1971.

Deschenes, C. L'actualisation de soi chez un groupe de religieuses, un groupe de femmes mariees et un groupe d'ex-religieuses. Unpublished masters thesis, University of Moncton, 1970.

Dick, L.D., & Ragland, R.E. A study of meditation in the service of counseling. Unpublished doctoral dissertation, University of Oklahoma, 1973.

Doress, I. A study of a sampling of Boston University student activists. Unpublished doctoral dissertation, Boston University, 1968.

Dossey, D.E. Effectiveness of a staff development program for elementary school principals in organizational development: Communications and basic human relations. Unpublished doctoral dissertation, Heed University, 1974.

Drude, K. A study of the construct validity of self-concept measures. Unpublished doctoral dissertation, University of Illinois, 1972.

Dumbauld, J.W. A comparison of counselor conditions offered in role playing with subsequent counselor conditions offered in practicum. Unpublished masters thesis, University of Florida, 1967.

Duncan, C.W. A comparison of certain experiences by life stages of selected groups of self-actualized, modal, and low-functioning college students. Unpublished doctoral dissertation, University of Florida, 1970.

Eatman, G.B. A correlation study between self-actualization and post-graduate aspirations. Unpublished masters thesis, Appalachian State University, 1972.

Eiben, R.E. Counselor-counselee personal orientation and post-interview affect. Unpublished doctoral dissertation, Ohio State University, 1968.

Elbert, W.E. Changes in self-concept, self-actualization, and interpersonal relations as a result of video feedback in sensitivity training. Unpublished doctoral dissertation, East Texas State University, 1969.

Fadem, P.R. Relationship between self-actualization and grade level preference of the elementary school teacher. Unpublished masters thesis, United States International University, 1971.

Fisher, I.S. The relationship between selected personality characteristics and the effects of training to develop small group productivity skills and interpersonal competence. *Dissertation Abstracts International*, Vol. XXXI, Number 4, 1970.

Fisher, T.L. A prediction of counselor facilitation from communication and discrimination indexes and a personality measure. Unpublished doctoral dissertation, University of Georgia, 1969.

Flanders, J.N. A humanistic approach to inservice education. Test results; Personal Orientation Inventory. Project Upper Cumberland, Title III ESEA, Overton County Board of Education Report, Livingston, Tennessee, 1969.

Ford, R.W. The relationship of psychological health of elementary school principals to the organizational climate of schools. Unpublished doctoral dissertation, Syracuse University, 1966.

Foulds, M.L. An investigation of the relationship between therapeutic conditions offered and a measure of self-actualization. Unpublished doctoral dissertation, University of Florida, 1967.

Fox, J. On the clinical use of the Personal Orientation Inventory (POI). Unpublished manuscript, 1965. (a)

Fox, J. Sex, age, hospitalization and self-actualization. Unpublished manuscript, 1965. (b)

Freedman, M.J. Homosexuality among women and psychological adjustment. Unpublished doctoral dissertation, Case Western Reserve University, 1967.

Freer, M.L. Counseling in supervision: Its place in helping student teachers toward greater autonomy. Unpublished doctoral dissertation, University of Idaho, 1972.

Gattshall, G.W. Imprisonment's effects upon the self-concept and the actualizing process. Unpublished doctoral dissertation, Ball State University, 1969.

Gerber, B.W. A study of relationships between psychological health and creativity. Unpublished doctoral dissertation, Syracuse University, 1964.

Gibb, L.L. A study of differences in sex, home background, educational background, work experience, extra curricular participation, and self-actualization attainment in college juniors. Unpublished doctoral dissertation, Northern Illinois University, 1966.

Gordon, R.D. A quantitative investigation of selected dynamics and outcomes of the basic encounter group. Unpublished doctoral dissertation, University of Kansas, 1971.

Grater, M.R. Effects of knowledge of characteristics of self-actualization and faking of a self-actualized response on Shostrom's Personal Orientation Inventory. Unpublished masters thesis, University of Toledo, 1968.

Greely, A.M. Personal communication, December 1970.

Green, R.V. Self-actualization measures and occupational aspiration. Unpublished doctoral dissertation, University of Kentucky, 1966.

Green, E.J. The relationship of self-actualization to achievement in nursing. Unpublished doctoral dissertation, Indiana University, 1967.

Grey, D.F. A study of terminators and remainers in treatment at a community health day center. Unpublished doctoral dissertation, United States International University, 1970.

Groeneveld, L.R. The positive experience group encounter and its effect upon self-actualization. Unpublished doctoral dissertation, Ball State University, 1969.

Gunnison, H. A study of the relationships of psychological health, political and economic attitudes and life values. Unpublished doctoral dissertation, Syracuse University, 1964.

Hall, E.A. Self-concept development of active and recovered alcoholics. Unpublished doctoral dissertation, University of Arizona, 1973.

Hannigan, P.S. An investigation of the comparative effects of a 16-hour and a 24-hour marathon gestalt workshop on a measure of self-actualization. Unpublished doctoral dissertation, The University of Toledo, 1975.

Hargadine, M.P. Relationships between measures of self-actualization and evaluation of scope of movement. Unpublished doctoral dissertation, University of Southern California, 1973.

Hayes, P.L., III. A study of the relationship of a measure of self-actualization to resident counselor effectiveness. Unpublished doctoral dissertation, University of Virginia, 1971.

Heaton, J.M. Adolescent orientation, achievement and family interaction. Unpublished doctoral dissertation, Florida State University, 1971.

Heckler, V.J. The contribution of psychological research to an understanding of the American priesthood: A study of a vocation under stress. Paper presented to the Annual Convention of the American Psychological Association, 1970.

Hersch, L.E. Self-actualization as it relates to the decision to have children. Unpublished masters thesis, United States International University, 1973.

Hood, W.D. Counselor-client similarity of self-actualization level and its relation to counseling outcome. Unpublished doctoral dissertation, Ball State University, 1968.

Hooge-Rochelle, J.E. The relationship between self-actualization and the role of married women. Unpublished masters thesis, United States International University, 1970.

Hoover, H.M.P. Concept development of college students exposed to systematic, organized learning experiences in family relationships. Unpublished doctoral dissertation. Oklahoma State University, 1966.

Hurd, D.E. The relationship of affective variables to college achievement. Unpublished doctoral dissertation, Indiana University, 1970.

Jackson, A.M. The effects of three group approaches in effecting change among black students. Unpublished doctoral dissertation, Indiana University, 1971.

Janssen, L. Inventario de Orientacion Personal para medir auto-actualizacion: Adaptacion y evaluacion. Unpublished masters thesis, University of Puerto Rico, 1975.

Jeffers, J.J.L. Effects of marathon encounter groups on personality characteristics of group members and group facilitators. Unpublished doctoral dissertation, University of Colorado, 1971.

Jenkins, F.S.H. Relationship of teacher characteristics to rapport between teachers and Mexican-American students. Unpublished doctoral dissertation, United States International University, 1970.

Jepson, P. Some effects of self-actualizing growth psychology on teenagers. United States International University, 1969. (Order No. 70-10, 416.)

Johnson, E.G., Jr. A comparison of academically successful and unsuccessful college of education freshmen on two measures of "self." Unpublished doctoral dissertation, University of Toledo, 1967.

Jones, L.K. Relationship between self-disclosure and positive mental health, modeled self-disclosure, and socioeconomic status. Unpublished doctoral dissertaton, University of Missouri, 1971.

Jorgenson, R.D. Relationship of teacher perception to student and teacher self-actualization. Unpublished doctoral dissertation, Ball State University, 1968.

Jury, L.E. Teacher self-actualization and pupil control ideology. *Dissertation Abstracts,* Vol. XXXIV, Number 8, 1974.

Kaats, B.A. Personality change as a function of group experience in a drug education and counseling program. Unpublished masters thesis, Trinity University, 1972.

Kammeier, M.L. Biographic, cognitive, demographic and personality differences between adolescents from families with identifiable alcohol problems and from families without identifiable alcohol problems. Unpublished doctoral dissertation, University of North Dakota, 1969.

Kelly, M.A. Active vs passive leadership techniques with development groups. Unpublished doctoral dissertation, University of Arizona, 1970.

Kilmann, P.R. The effects of structure of marathon group therapy and locus of control on therapeutic outcome. Unpublished doctoral dissertation, Brigham Young University, 1973.

Kilmann, P.R., Albert, B.M., & Sotile, W.M. The relationship between locus of control, structure of therapy, and outcome: A replication of Kilmann and Howell (1974). Unpublished manuscript, University of South Carolina.

Kilmann, P.R., Follingstad, D.R., Price, M.G., Rowland, K.F., & Robinson, E.A. Marathon group therapy, self-actualization, and attitudes toward women. Unpublished manuscript, University of South Carolina.

Kleiner, F.B. Personality and training: Their effects on the communication of empathy. Unpublished doctoral dissertation, Ohio State University, 1970.

Klingberg, H.E., Jr. An evaluation of sensitivity training effects on self-actualization, purpose in life, and religious attitudes of theological students. Unpublished doctoral dissertation, Fuller Theological Seminary, 1971.

Korski, L.C. Effects of growth group experiences on adolescents' purpose in life, self-concept, and self-actualization. Unpublished masters thesis, United States International University, 1973.

Kremers, M.A. A comparison of members of Alcoholics Anonymous with practicing alcoholics and selected samples of nonalcoholics, in terms of a positive concept of mental health. Unpublished manuscript, 1974.

Krouner, P.J. The relationship between teacher psychological health and acceptance of the paraprofessional. Unpublished doctoral dissertation, Syracuse University, 1970.

Kuehn, W.L. Self-actualization and engagement-involvement response to literature among adolescents. Unpublished doctoral dissertation, University of Minnesota, 1973.

LaBach, P. Self-actualization in college students: Interrelationships of self-actualization, personal characteristics, and attitudes in subcultures of liberal arts freshmen and seniors. Unpublished doctoral dissertation, Kent State University, 1969. (On Microfilm Order No. 70-16, 536.)

Ladenberger, M.E. An analysis of self-actualizing dimensions of top and middle management personnel. *Dissertation Abstracts International*, Vol. XXXII, Number 1, 1971.

Lamb, D.W. Demonstrated internal-external reward expectancies as a variable in group counseling. Unpublished doctoral dissertation, North Texas State University, 1968.

Lamott, J.R. A study of personal value orientations associated with anticipated career specialty choices of a population of medical students. Unpublished doctoral dissertation, University of Washington, 1968.

Lavoie, D. Phenomenological transformation of the self-concept toward self-actualization through sensitivity training laboratory. Paper read at the Psychological Association of the Philippines meeting, 1971.

Leatherwood, H.W. The effectiveness of small-group procedures in the classroom as aids in movement toward self-actualization in junior college students. Unpublished doctoral dissertation, East Texas State University, 1971.

Lee, R.J. Correlates of interest maturity. Unpublished doctoral dissertation, Western Reserve University, 1965.

Lewis, S.O. A test of small-group procedures in college adjustment. Unpublished doctoral dissertation, University of Kentucky, 1968.

Libenson, M.A. Relationship of academic performance to perceptual congruence between selected college freshmen and their parents. Unpublished doctoral dissertation, Boston University, 1969.

Lo, S.N. Effects of self-reinforcement and goal-setting on the affect and personal orientation of housewives. Unpublished doctoral dissertation, Fuller Theological Seminary, 1971.

Lovekin, A. The effects upon the outcome of a human relations institute of generalized expectancies for internal versus external control of reinforcement. Unpublished masters research, Fuller Theological Seminary, 1972.

Low, G.R. A study of counselor trainee changes in two types of practicum. Unpublished doctoral dissertation, East Texas State University, 1969.

Luzzi, M.A.H. A study of the relationship of self-acceptance and social values to effectiveness of male rehabilitation counselor trainees. Unpublished doctoral dissertation, Boston University, 1970.

Mace, R.E. Factors influencing the decisions of teachers to become administrators: A study of the differences in self-actualization and job satisfaction occurring between future administrators and career teachers. Unpublished doctoral dissertation, Syracuse University, 1970.

Macklin, T.J. Interpersonal communication and self-actualization. Unpublished masters thesis, University of Wisconsin, 1973.

Margulies, N. A study of organizational culture and the self-actualizing process. Unpublished doctoral dissertation, University of California, Los Angeles, 1965.

Margulis, M. Perceptual and cognitive correlates of self-actualization. Unpublished doctoral dissertation, University of Maine, 1971.

Marshall, S.W. Parent child-rearing attitudes and psychological health of the parent. Unpublished doctoral dissertation, Syracuse University, 1966.

Masucci, M.J. Psychological health and occupational perceptions in a selected sample. Unpublished doctoral dissertation, Syracuse University, 1966.

Maul, T.L. An investigation of the relationships between self-actualization and creative thinking processes. Unpublished doctoral dissertation, University of California at Berkeley, 1970.

McCabe, O.L. An empirical investigation of the effects of chemically (LSD-25)-induced "psychedelic experiences" on selected measures of personality, and their implications for therapeutic counseling theory and practice. *Dissertation Abstracts International*, Vol. xXIX, Number 12, 1969.

McKissick, G.C. The relationship among the factors of academic ability, self-actualization, and achievement of seniors in a four-year liberal arts college for women. Unpublished doctoral dissertation, University of Missouri, 1975.

McLoone, G.W. Relationships between a measure of anxiety and aspects of self-actualization, with implications for vocational choice and vocational counseling. Unpublished masters thesis, Catholic University of America, 1968.

Melchers, E.E. The value of the Personal Orientation Inventory in predicting counselor effectiveness and the value of a counseling practicum in promoting self-actualization. Unpublished doctoral dissertation, University of Northern Colorado, 1971.

Miller, J.H. Sensitivity training with incarcerated criminals: Personality correlates of participant duration and an assessment of therapeutic value. Unpublished doctoral dissertation, Auburn University, 1971.

Miller, R.R. A study of self-actualization in an introduction to education course. Unpublished doctoral dissertation, Case Western Reserve University, 1972.

Moritz, F.C. A human relations laboratory as an inservice education program. Unpublished doctoral dissertation, Arizona State University, 1969.

Morris, J.D. The effects of counselor and client inner-directedness on the development of attitudes toward the counseling relationship. Unpublished dissertation, Indiana University, 1971.

Munden, J.R. An analysis of a master of education program in counseling and guidance through a follow-up of graduates. Unpublished doctoral dissertation, Saint Louis University, 1970.

Murphy, C. The effects of relaxation on the training of counselors. Unpublished masters thesis, University of Moncton, 1972.

Murphy, T.J. The relationship between self-actualization and adjustment among American Catholic priests. Unpublished masters thesis, Loyola University, 1972.

Murray, M.E. An exploration of the relationship of self-actualization to teacher success. Unpublished masters thesis, Pennsylvania State University, 1966.

Murray, M.E. Self-actualization and social values of teachers as related to students perception of teachers. Unpublished doctoral dissertation, Pennsylvania State University, 1968.

Oas, P.C. Drug use as related to expressing or receiving affection and anger. Unpublished doctoral dissertation, United States International University, 1971.

Ohlbaum, J.S. Self-concepts, value characteristics, and self-actualization of professional and non-professional women. Unpublished doctoral dissertation, United States International University, 1970.

Oliver, C.M. A study of the effects of behavioral group counseling on self-actualization. Unpublished doctoral dissertation, University of Southern Mississippi, 1970.

Otto, B.M. Anxiety, creativity and self-actualization. Unpublished masters thesis, California State College, Long Beach, 1967.

Pandal, F.G. A cross-cultural exploratory study of self-actualization in American and Mexican students. Unpublished masters thesis, San Fernando Valley State College, 1972.

Pearson, O. Effects of group guidance upon college adjustment. Unpublished doctoral dissertation, University of Kentucky, 1966.

Pellegrin, V.B.H. A descriptive study of a Midwestern sample of Episcopal clergy and seminarians categorized according to various criteria. Unpublished doctoral dissertation, University of Kansas, 1970.

Penner, C.L. The effectiveness of a theologically oriented approach to lay counselor training. Unpublished doctoral dissertation, Fuller Theological Seminary, 1971.

Pines, R.A. Some affective and cognitive outcomes in an introductory teacher-education course under conditions of student centered and instructor centered study. Unpublished doctoral dissertation, University of Miami, 1970.

Pitts, G.D. Values, attitudes, opinions, and concerns of subcultures of concerned students in an urban commuter college. Unpublished doctoral dissertation, Northwestern University, 1970.

Poe, B.J. The effect of sensitivity training on the relationship between risk taking and other selected behavioral factors. Unpublished doctoral dissertation, East Texas State University, 1971.

Post, A.W. Deprivation of opportunity: Industrial mental health and job behavior. Unpublished doctoral dissertation, Case Western Reserve University, 1971.

Post, H.H., Jr. Self-actualization and the interpersonal relationship environment. Unpublished doctoral dissertation, Boston University, 1969.

Provost, R.L. A follow-up study of beginning teachers in multi-cultural schools who have attended a pre-service institute dealing with problems of school disintegration. Unpublished doctoral dissertation, East Texas State University, 1970.

Puishes, D.S. Self-actualization and facilitative interpersonal communication: Their relationship and roles in the selection and training of counselors and therapists. Unpublished masters thesis, San Jose State University, 1975.

Reekie, E. Personality factors and biographical characteristics associated with criterion behaviors of success in professional nursing. Unpublished doctoral dissertation, University of Washington, 1970.

Reschke, S.E. Mental health factors in college students: A test of the motivation-hygiene theory. Unpublished doctoral dissertation, Western Reserve University, 1967.

Reynolds, E.N. Interpersonal risk and self-actualization in four religious groups. Unpublished doctoral dissertation, Case Western Reserve University, 1968.

Ridge, R.A. Self-actualization, achievement and other factors as a function of college students in selected housing settings. Unpublished doctoral dissertation, University of Florida, 1968.

Roberts, J.E. Self-actualization and the effectiveness of two patterns of supervision. Unpublished doctoral dissertation, University of Wisconsin, 1972.

Rogers, M.I. Self-actualization as process. Unpublished doctoral dissertation, Case Western Reserve University, 1968.

Rohaly, K.A. The relationships between movement participation, movement satisfaction, self-actualization, and trait anxiety in selected college freshman women. Unpublished doctoral dissertation, Ohio State University, 1971.

Romano, R.J. Counseling outcomes related to family background of delinquent male adolescents. Unpublished doctoral dissertation, Boston University, 1970.

Rosenthal, J.C. A study of the self-actualizing process of selected university freshmen women students. Unpublished doctoral dissertation, Colorado State College, 1967.

Rowe, W. The effect of short-term group counseling and cognitive learning on a measure of self-actualization of counselors in training. Unpublished doctoral dissertation, Michigan State University, 1971.

Royer, J.P. Self-concept rigidity vs. age measured by selected scales of the Personal Orientation Inventory. Unpublished Masters Thesis, San Jose State University, 1974.

Rubin, H.S. The prevention of student attrition in nursing education: A community psychology approach. Unpublished doctoral dissertation, Illinois Institute of Technology, 1971.

Russell, W.J.C. A study of changes in measures of inner-direction, openminedness, and intraception during laboratory training designs of the Methodist Church. Unpublished doctoral dissertation, Syracuse University, 1968.

Rutschmann, D.F. Affective versus cognitive groups with pre-college blind youth. Urbana, Ill.: University of Illinois at Urbana, 1970. (On Microfilm.)

Salva, D.M. Self-actualization and its relationship to intensity of vocational interests of male college freshmen. Unpublished doctoral dissertation, University of Kansas, 1968.

Sands, B.L. An exploratory study of self-actualization and self-perception of competency among Michigan family life teachers. Unpublished doctoral dissertation, Michigan State University, 1970.

Schenk, K.N. Factors associated with planned change in Baccalaureate nursing programs. Unpublished doctoral dissertation, University of Florida, 1969.

Schmidt, M. Effects of group interaction on the self-perceptions of religious women. Unpublished doctoral dissertation. University of Illinois, 1970.

Schmitt, A.F. A measure of self-actualization of the naval aviator. Unpublished masters thesis, United States International University, 1973.

Schroeder, B.L.F. An examination of the characteristics of students and faculty in a small, black, denominational college. Unpublished doctoral dissertation, University of Texas, 1970.

Shafer, B.W. A study of behavioral and perceptual changes in counselor trainees as a result of resident and nonresident practicum programs. Unpublished doctoral dissertation, East Texas State University, 1970.

Sherman, L.L. Movers and perserverers in education: An investigation of interests, values, personality factors, self-actualizations, need satisfaction and job satisfaction among movers into counseling and into administration and among perserverers in teaching. Unpublished doctoral dissertation, New York University, 1969.

Shimmin, E.L. A study of the dimensions of self-actualization of staff nurses in a visiting nurse agency in a New England city. Unpublished masters thesis, University of Washington, 1969.

Simmons, N.C. A study of the relationsihp between Shostrom's manipulative diagnostic system and Personal Orientation Inventory. Unpublished masters thesis, University of South Carolina, 1969.

Smith, J.A. The prediction of academic success from self-actualizing values. Unpublished doctoral thesis, Shippensburg State College, 1973.

Smith, M.L.H. The facilitation of student self-directed learning as perceived by teachers with high and low levels of self-actualization and dogmatism. Unpublished doctoral dissertation, Pennsylvania State University, 1968.

Smith, O.P., Jr. Changes in self-actualization and self-concept as a result of the use of visual feedback in marathon sensitivity training. Unpublished doctoral dissertation, East Texas State University, 1970.

Spikes, S. The relationship between the POI, SAI, and self-disclosure. Unpublished masters thesis, Trinity University, 1972.

Squatriglia, R.W. The impact of short-term group counseling on student values. Unpublished doctoral dissertation, University of South Carolina, 1970.

Starrett, R.H. Improving the specific trait prediction of the *Personal Orientation Inventory*. Unpublished masters thesis, Ohio State University, 1973.

Stein, F. Consistency of cognitive, interest, and personality variables with academic mastery: A study of field-dependence-independence verbal comprehension, self-perception, and vocational interest in relation to academic performance among male juniors attending an urban university. Unpublished doctoral dissertation, New York University, 1968.

Sterchele, N.R. An investigation of some relationships between self-actualization and child-centeredness among teachers. Unpublished doctoral dissertation, Michigan State University, 1973.

Stockton, R.A. An investigation of the effect of sensitivity training on the attitudes of teacher education training. Unpublished doctoral dissertation, Ball State University, 1969.

Stout, R.J. A study of alienation on three diverse Ohio college campuses. Unpublished doctoral dissertation, Bowling Green State University, 1970.

Swift, M.S. Parent child-rearing attitudes and psychological health of the parent. Unpublished doctoral dissertation, Syracuse University, 1966.

Tallant, W.J. Changes in pre-service teachers involved in a multi-cultural training program utilizing formal presentations, sensitivity training, planned social activities, and a cooperative living arrangement. Unpublished doctoral dissertation, East Texas State University, 1970.

Theriault, P.J. Relation de certaines variables socio-demographiques avec l'actualisation de soi chez un groupe de candidats a jeunesse canada/monde. Unpublished masters thesis, Université de Moncton, N.B. Canada, 1973.

Thompson, S.A. A study of the relationship between personality factors of counselors and counselee perceptions of these counselors. Unpublished doctoral dissertation, Auburn University, 1968.

Thompson, S.D. A measure of self-actualization (Personal Orientation Inventory) of student teachers of guidance. Unpublished doctoral dissertation, University of British Columbia, 1968.

Thurston, B.L. A comparison of selected psychological health factors and perceptions of administrative procedures in those ministers and seminary students perceiving the administrative role to be more integral to an effective ministry and those perceiving that role to be less integral. Unpublished doctoral dissertation, Syracuse University, 1970. (a)

Thurston, B.L. Psychological health and its relationship to ministers' perception of their administrative role. Paper read at American Academy of Religion, 1970. (b)

Tremblay, B. Les caracteristiques de la personne et du comportement du professeur de niveau collegial, favorisant un a-prentissage existentiel par l'etudiant. Unpublished doctoral dissertation, University of British Columbia, 1968.

Trueblood, R.W., & McHolland, J.D. Measure of change toward self-actualization through the human potential group process. Unpublished manuscript, 1971.

Tucker, F.C., Jr. A study of the relationships between: (1) Teachers' level of self-actualization and their teaching behavioral styles, and (2) Teachers' teaching behavioral styles and the gratifications they derive from interacting with their students. Unpublished doctoral dissertation, Syracuse University, 1970.

Tueller, R.L. The use of personality traits in predicting doctoral student success at Utah State University. Unpublished doctoral dissertation, Utah State University, 1971.

Vaughan, J.L. Measurement and analysis of values pertaining to psychotherapy and mental health. Unpublished doctoral dissertation, Columbia University, 1971.

Walker, N.P. Clothing expenditures as related to selected values, self-actualization, and buying practices: An exploratory study. Unpublished doctoral dissertation, Pennsylvania State University, 1968.

Walton, O. Social conformity, emotional maturity and self-perception. Unpublished masters thesis, Saint Louis University, 1973.

Weber, M.S. A study of the relationship between ability grouping and personality traits of high school girls. Unpublished doctoral dissertation, Loyola University, 1970.

Webster, A.C. Patterns and relationships of dogmatism, mental health and psychological health in selected religious groups. Unpublished doctoral dissertation, Syracuse University, 1966.

Weck, E.-E. The relationship of sexual functioning to inner/other directedness. Unpublished masters thesis, West Georgia College, 1974.

Weinrach, S.G. The relationship between the level of counselor self-actualization and student perception of the guidance program. Unpublished doctoral dissertation, University of Toledo, 1972.

Weir, W.R. The use of a measure of self-actualization in the treatment of alcoholics and their spouses in an out-patient agency. Unpublished masters thesis, University of North Dakota, 1965.

Weis, S.J.F. An exploratory study of the nature of the occurrence of creativity and self-actualization among college students making vocational selections in the home economics field. Unpublished masters thesis, Pennsylvania State University, 1966.

Wesch, J.E. Self-actualization and the fear of death. Unpublished doctoral dissertation, University of Tennessee, 1970.

White, H.M. An investigation of some characteristics of high and low self-actualization and their relationship to alienation from self and society. Unpublished doctoral dissertation, University of California at Berkeley, 1970.

Whitsett, D.A. Self-actualization and the modern formal organization. Unpublished doctoral dissertation, Western Reserve University, 1967.

Yeager, J.C. The effectiveness of a training program in human relations. Unpublished doctoral dissertation, University of Pittsburgh, 1969.

Zimmerman, W.S., Abou Ghorra, I.J., Fox, J., Michael, W.B., & Shostrom, E.L. The measurement of self-actualization. Symposium presented to the California State Psychological Association, Newport Beach, California, 1969.

SUPPLEMENTARY REFERENCES

Bach, G.R., & Goldberg, H. *Creative Aggression.* Garden City, N.Y.: Doubleday, 1974.

Brown, G.I. *Human teaching for human learning: An introduction to confluent education.* New York: Viking, 1971.

Buhler, C. *Values in psychotherapy.* New York: Free Press of Glencoe, 1962.

Campbell, D., & Fiske, D.W. Convergent and discriminant validation by the multitrait-multimethod matrix. *Psychological Bulletin*, 1959, 50, 81-105.

Carkhuff, R.R. *Helping and human relations, A primer for lay and professional helpers.* Vol. 1, *Selection and training.* New York: Holt, Rinehart & Winston, 1969.

Cattell, R.B. The 16PF and basic personality structure. *Journal of Behavioral Science,* 1972, 1, 169-187.

Cattell, R.B., & Eber, H.W. *The sixteen personality factor questionnaire.* Champaign, Ill.: Institute for Personality and Ability Testing, 1957.

Cattell, R.B., Eber, H.W., & Tatsouka, M.M. *Handbook for the Sixteen Personality Factor Questionnaire.* Champaign, Ill.: Institute for Personality and Ability Testing, 1970.

Comrey, A.L. *Comrey personality scales.* San Diego: EdITS, 1970.

Cook, W.W., Leeds, C.H., & Callis, R. *Minnesota teacher attitude inventory.* New York: Psychological Corporation, 1953.

Crowne, D.P., &Marlowe, D. A new scale of social desirability independent of psychopathology. *Journal of Consutling Psychology,* 1960, 24, 349-354.

Crumbaugh, J., & Maholick, L. *Manual of instructions for the Purpose in Life Test.* Munster, Ind.: Psychometric Affiliates, 1969.

Drucker, P. *Principles of management.* New York: Harper & Row, 1954.

Dymond, R.F. Adjustment changes over therapy from self-sorts. In Rogers, C., & Dymond, R. (eds.), *Psychotherapy and personality change.* Chicago: University of Chicago Press, 1954.

Edwards, A.L. *Edwards personal preference schedule.* New York: Psychological Corporation, 1959.

Ellis, A. *Reason and emotion in psychotherapy.* New York: Lyle Stuart, 1962.

Eysenck, H.J. *The inequality of man.* San Diego: EdITS, 1975.

Eysenck, H.J., & Eysenck, S. *The Eysenck personality inventory. San Diego: EdITS, 1963.*

Eysenck, H.J., & Eysenck, S. *Eysenck personality questionnaire.* San Diego: EdITS, 1975.

Frankl, V. *Man's search for meaning.* New York: Simon & Schuster, 1963.

Frankl, V. Self-transcedence as a human phenomenon. *Journal of Humanistic Psychology,* 1966, *Fall*, 97-106.

Gibb, J.R. Sensitivity training as a medium for personal growth and improved interpersonal relationships. In Egan, G. (ed.), *Encounter groups: Basic readings.* Belmont, Calif.: Wadsworth, 1971.

Gordon, L.V. *Gordon personal inventory.* New York: Harcourt Brace Jovanovich, 1956.

Greeley, A. Personal communication, December 31, 1970.
Guilford, J.P. When not to factor analyze. *Psychological Bulletin,* 1952, 49, 26-37.
Guilford, J.P., & Zimmerman, W.S. *Guilford-Zimmerman temperament survey.* Los Angeles: Sheridan Psychological Services, 1949.
Hathaway, S.R., & McKinley, J.C. *Minnesota multiphasic personality inventory.* New York: The Psychological Corporation, 1951.
Hilgard, E.R., & Atkinson, R.E. *Introduction to psychology.* New York: Harcourt Brace Jovanovich, 1967.
Jellinek, E.M. *The disease concept of alcoholism.* New Haven, Conn.: College & University Press, 1960.
Jones, J.P. Changing patterns of leadership. *Personnel,* 1967, 44, 8-15.
Kerlinger, F.N. *Foundations of behavioral research.* New York: Holt, Rinehart & Winston, 1973.
Knapp, R.R. Encounter group experience and self-actualization. *EdITS Research and Developments,* 1973, 2, 1-4.
Maslow, A.H. *Toward a psychology of being.* New York: Van Nostrand, 1962.
Maslow, A.H. *Eupsychian management.* Homewood, Ill.: Dorsey Press, 1965.
Maslow, A.H. *Motivation and personality.* New York: Harper & Row, 1970.
Maslow, A.H. *The farther reaches of human nature.* New York: Viking, 1971.
May, R., Angel, T., & Ellenberger, H. *Existence.* New York: Basic Books, 1958.
Mednick, S.A., & Mednick, M.T. *Remote associates test.* Boston: Houghton Mifflin, 1967.
Milam, J.R. *The emergent comprehensive concept of alcoholism. Kirkland, Wash.: Alcoholism Center Associates Press, 1974.*
Neff, W.S. *Work and human behavior.* New York: Atherton Press, 1968.
Ommanny, P.C., & Fifield, M.R. The measurement of self-actualization. Unpublished doctoral dissertation, United States International University, 1973.
Peele, S., & Brodsky, A. *Love and addiction.* New York: Taplinger, 1975.
Perls, F. *Ego, hunger and aggression.* London: George Allen and Unwin, 1947.
Perls, F., Hefferline, R., & Goodman, P. *Gestalt therapy.* New York: Julian, 1951.
Perls, F. *The gestalt approach & eye witness to therapy.* Palo Alto, Calif.: Science & Behavior Books, 1973.
Pfeiffer, J.W., & Heslin, R. *Instrumentation in human relations training.* San Diego: University Associates, 1973.
Riesman, D., Glazer, N., & Denny, R. *The lonely crowd.* New York: Doubleday, 1950.
Rogers, C. *Client-centered therapy.* Boston: Houghton Mifflin, 1951.

Rogers, C. The characteristics of a helping relationship. *Personnel and Guidance Journal,* 1958, 37, 6-15.

Rogers, C. Interpersonal relationships: U.S.A. 2000. *Journal of Applied Behavioral Science,* 1968, 4, 265-280.

Rotter, J.B. Generalized expectancies for internal versus external control of reinforcement. *Psychological Monographs,* 1966, 80(1).

Smith, N.R. *The entrepreneur and his firm.* East Lansing, Mich.: Bureau of Business and Economic Research, Graduate School of Business Administration, Michigan State University, 1967.

Thurstone, L.L. *Multiple factor analysis.* Chicago: University of Chicago Press, 1947.

Tsujioka, B., & Cattell, R.B. The importance of factor-trueness and validity, versus homogeneity and orthogonality, in test scales. *Educational Psychological Measurement,* 1964, 24, 3-30.

Weil, A. *The natural mind.* Boston: Houghton Mifflin, 1972.

Yalom, I.D., & Lieberman, M.A. A study of encounter group casualties. *Archives of General Psychiatry,* 1971, 25, 16-30.

Zuckerman, M., & Lubin, B. *Multiple affect adjective check list.* San Diego: EdITS, 1965.

INDEX